Family-Friendly Ideas Your Church Can Do

Group

Loveland, Colorado

family-friendly Ideas Your Church Can Do

Copyright © 1998 Group Publishing, Inc.

Credits

Contributing Writers: Ben F. Freudenburg, Tim Kurth, Michael W. Sciarra, Liz Shockey, Kathy Sizer, and Bob Buller
Editor: Bob Buller
Chief Creative Officer: Joani Schultz
Copy Editor: Julie Meiklejohn
Art Director: Kari K. Monson
Cover Art Director: Jeff A. Storm
Computer Graphic Artist: Nighthawk Design
Cover Designer: Diana Walters
Illustrator: Amy Bryant
Production Manager: Gingar Kunkel

Library of Congress Cataloging-in-Publication Data
Family-friendly ideas your church can do.
   p. cm.
    ISBN 0-7644-2035-6 (alk. paper)
    1. Church work with families. I. Group Publishing.
  BV4438.F336   1997
  259.1--dc21   97-32379
                                            CIP

10 9 8 7 6 5 4 3 2   07 06 05 04 03 02 01 00 99 98
Printed in the United States of America.

Contents

Enrichment Activities

Fun Times

Introduction

Interest in family ministry has skyrocketed over the past few years, but the concept has been around for a long time. For years, churches have offered a wide variety of family ministry programs and services: premarital counseling for engaged couples, marriage retreats, parenting classes, even Sunday school classes that teach children of all ages to love God and obey their parents.

With few exceptions, these family ministry programs shared a common (though unrecognized) assumption: that the most effective way to serve families was to minister to the *individuals* in those families. More often than not, family ministry programs separated parents from children and attempted to meet the needs of each in age-graded (sometimes gender-defined) classes.

Valid though this approach may be in some cases, it is not the only way to conduct family ministry. Many churches today realize that effective family ministry teaches and guides family members as individuals *and* the family as a unit. Gone are the days of family members scattering in all directions every time the family walks through the church doors. Today more churches are offering family-friendly events in which family members learn, worship, and laugh together.

Of course, this change in approach to family ministry has placed new demands on church leaders. The need for family-based learning, worship, service, enrichment, and fun ideas has never been greater—which is exactly why this book was created. *Family-Friendly Ideas Your Church Can Do* gives you the resources you need to minister to the families in your church in the most effective way possible.

In *Family-Friendly Ideas Your Church Can Do,* you'll find learning activities to help family members read and talk about God's Word together; worship experiences in which family members honor God together; service projects that challenge and equip family members to serve God, others, and each other together; enrichment activities to draw family members closer to each other and to God; and fun times that will leave everyone wishing that every night were family fun night. In short, *Family-Friendly Ideas Your Church Can Do* gives you the tools to minister to the families in your congregation as *families* and not just as individuals who happen to drive to church together.

As you use the ideas in this book, you may want to keep in mind the following suggestions:

• **Recognize that you can create a family-friendly church without organizing a formal family ministry program.** Many churches do not have the resources to hire a family minister or to allocate large amounts of money to family ministry. But every church can offer family ministry. Simply use the ideas in this book to minister to families as families, and you'll find that you've created a family-friendly church in the process.

- **Recruit families to help you plan and prepare these activities.** The most effective family ministry programs don't rely on one or two people to do all the work. Effective family ministry encourages *families* to do things together. So invite families to help plan and prepare family-friendly events and activities for others to enjoy.

- **Be sure to include families of all shapes and sizes.** A number of families in your church probably don't fit the stereotypical family mold (one or more children living with their biological parents). To create a truly family-friendly environment, you need to accept and minister to families where they are, not where you wish they were. So make a special effort to minister to every family in your church, regardless of its shape or size.

- **Look for creative ways to include singles and couples without children at home.** Ideally, the church as a whole will operate as an extended family that includes and involves every valued member. So sensitively invite and include anyone who might want to attend or to help with your family-friendly events. Remember: There's a place for everyone in God's family.

- **Use these family-friendly ideas for special family events *and* as a part of your regular church program.** Many churches schedule a special "family night" once a week or once a month. This approach provides an easy and effective way to minister to church families, but you can accomplish far more by using these ideas during regular church events as well. Occasionally incorporating a family-friendly activity into a Sunday evening service, an all-church social, or even a Sunday morning worship time is an effective way to advertise your family-friendly focus and to demonstrate your belief that the church as a whole is a family.

So use (and adapt) the learning, worship, service, enrichment, and fun ideas that follow to create a family-friendly environment in which family members grow closer to each other and to God.

Learning Activities

Family Friendship Quilt

Family Focus: Families will create "friendship quilts" as they learn about the building blocks of family friendships.

Supplies: You'll need Bibles, eight-inch-square pieces of light-colored fabric, and permanent markers. You'll need nine fabric squares for each family that attends.

Have members of each family sit in a circle on the floor and each think of a best friend outside of the family. Then ask each family member to name the best friend and to explain why he or she is close to that person.

After several minutes, say: **One of the good things that God gives us is**

....

Family-Friendly Advice

To simplify your preparations, ask each family to bring its own quilt blocks. However, be sure to provide extras in case anyone forgets to bring quilt blocks.
....

close friends. But God also wants us to be close friends with the members of our families. So today we're going to talk about the building blocks of friendship, whether it's with people outside of our families or with the members of our families. To help us remember what it takes to be a friend, we are going to start to make family friendship quilts you can finish at home during the coming week.

Set out the supplies. Invite families each to take nine quilt blocks (if they didn't bring their own), Bibles, and markers.

When family groups have their supplies, ask family members to read Proverbs 10:12 together. Then ask:

- **How do you think love builds friendship with others?**
- **How has your best friend shown God's love to you?**
- **How can you show God's love to your family members?**

Then have family members work together to draw and color in a red heart on one quilt block.

After several minutes, have family members read Ephesians 4:25 together and then discuss the following questions:

- **How does honesty build friendship with others?**
- **How has your best friend been honest with you?**
- **How can you be honest with the members of your family?**

Have family members work together to draw a ruler (symbolizing "measuring up to the truth") on a second quilt block.

After several minutes, ask family members to read Romans 15:7 together and then have them discuss the following questions:

- **How does acceptance build friendship with others?**
- **How has your best friend shown acceptance to you?**
- **How can you show acceptance to the members of your family?**

Then have family members work together to draw a pair of open hands on a third quilt block.

After several minutes, have family members read Ephesians 4:3-6 together and then discuss the following questions:

- **How does faith in God build friendship with others?**
- **How might a best friend's faith in God build friendship?**
- **How can your family's faith draw you closer together as a family?**

Then have family members work together to draw and color in a cross on a fourth quilt block.

After several minutes, say: **Love, honesty, acceptance, and faith in God are four building blocks that help us build solid friendships with people outside of our families and with our own family members. Let's finish our quilt blocks by drawing pictures that portray how we can apply each of these building blocks within our families.**

Encourage family members to think of one way they can practice each characteristic within their family and then draw a picture of each idea on a separate quilt block. If families have trouble drawing their ideas, suggest that they write short phrases that will remind them of what they can do.

Then have each family commit to building true friendship within the family by writing its last name in the center of the remaining quilt block and each family member's first name around the edges of that block. Conclude with a prayer asking God to help the members of each family become closer together as true friends. Instruct families to assemble their quilts at home by sewing together the quilt blocks and then sewing a sheet or a soft blanket to the back of the quilt.

Taking It Home

Suggest that families add more blocks to their quilts, some just for decoration and others to represent the building blocks of friendship. Families might add blocks for trust, respect, sharing, or serving one another. Encourage family members to talk about which of the traits they already have in their families and which they need to work on.

Helpers in God's Church

Family Focus: Families will learn how others serve in your church and how they might serve as well.

Supplies: You'll need a church map showing the places families will explore and the supplies listed for each of the four learning stations described below.

One week prior to the meeting, arrange with your church workers to set up the following learning stations:

- a custodian with his or her tools and enough supplies for each family member to participate in a simple custodial task.
- an usher with offering plates and pictures of what the money collected goes toward.
- a deacon (or your church's equivalent) with either (1) a grocery bag of food for the needy and materials to make cards for shut-ins or (2) Communion

utensils, the equipment used to fill the cups, and various breads to taste.

family-friendly Advice

If you prefer, substitute the learning stations described with ones more appropriate for your church, such as a choir leader with songs for families to sing, a video or sound-system operator with dials to turn, or a secretary with office tasks for families to complete.

- an elder or a church decision-maker with a copy of a decision to role play.

As much as possible, locate the stations where workers usually perform their duties: the usher in the entry of the worship area, the elder in a church meeting room, and so on. Tell the workers that they will each have fifteen minutes to explain what they do at church and to lead families in a relevant activity. Suggest the following ideas for the learning stations (adapt the ideas as needed to reflect the jobs actually performed in your church):

- The custodian might display the various tools used around the church and then have families perform a simple custodial task such as washing windows, dusting pews, straightening hymnals, or some other simple task younger kids can perform.

- The usher might explain how ushers in your church collect the offering, show pictures of what the money goes toward, and let family members practice taking up an offering.

- Depending on the deacon's role in your church, the deacon could (1) point out a bag of groceries, explain that deacons visit and take food to people in need, and ask members of each family to work together to make a card for the deacon to take with him or her on a visit or (2) demonstrate how Communion cups are filled, allow each person to fill a cup, and explain the type of bread used in the Lord's Supper at your church. (If your tradition permits it, you might also let family members taste different kinds of bread to compare them to the bread used in the Lord's Supper.)

- The elder (or a member of your church's decision-making group) might explain how decisions are made in your church and challenge family members to role play making a decision. For example, family members might decide how to use a $1 million gift to the church. Do they build a new gym, remodel the sanctuary and classrooms, send it to missionaries, build a shelter to feed and house homeless people, or spend it in some other way?

As families arrive, give them church maps showing where each learning station may be found. Explain that members of each family will go through four learning stations together to learn how various people serve in God's church. Families may spend up to fifteen minutes at each station and then move on to a new station. Instruct families to return to your meeting area in one hour even if they haven't finished every station. Then encourage family groups to scatter among the stations so no station becomes overly crowded.

Circulate among the stations, and remind people to move to new stations every fifteen minutes. At the end of the hour, encourage families to return to your meeting area.

After everyone has returned, ask each family to form a group and read 1 Corinthians 12:27 and 21. Then have each family discuss the following questions:

- **In what ways is a church like a body? How is it different?**
- **What would happen if our bodies lost some of their parts?**
- **What would happen if our church lost some of its workers?**
- **What are some ways our family could serve in the church?**

Close in prayer, thanking God for all the workers in your church and asking God to show everyone present how he or she can be a part of God's work in the church.

Taking It Home

Invite each family to choose one task that family members can perform together at church. For example, one family might agree to fill in for the ushers one Sunday a month, while another family might commit to shopping for the groceries your church distributes. Encourage families to rotate their service commitments so everyone can learn of the various needs within your church.

The House That Love Built

Family Focus: Family members will build and tear apart block houses as they learn to build up and not destroy their families.

Supplies: You'll need Bibles and building materials such as dominoes, cards, blocks, sugar cubes, or toy "logs." You'll also need an instant-print camera and enough film to take a picture of each group.

Set the building supplies on a central table. Then ask members of each family to gather around a table. Invite singles and couples without children to form groups of three or four. Have each group select some building materials, at least three or four pieces per group member. Explain that groups will want to choose materials suited for the building of a house.

Once groups have selected their materials and returned to their tables, say: **Before you start constructing your houses, let's take a look at Romans 15:1-2. Read it together in your group and then use the materials you**

have to build a house. Take turns adding one block or card at a time until you have built the sturdiest house you can. Be sure to have each person participate.

Give families and groups five minutes to work on their houses. When most of the houses are complete, say: **It looks like you've all built sturdy little houses. Good job! But how well do you think they would stand up under pressure? To find out, take turns within your group saying things that would "tear down" a happy home. You might use phrases such as "I won't clean my room" or "No. You can't go, and I don't want to talk about it." Think of things that you actually say or do that make other family members feel sad or hurt. As each person makes a "destructive" statement, have him or her remove a block from the house.**

Allow five minutes for groups to demolish their buildings. When all the groups have disassembled their buildings, say: **When we say or do anything that does not help others, we tear them down. Little by little, we take our homes apart with negative attitudes and words. Let's read Romans 15:1-2 again and think about ways we can try to please others so that they will be built up. As you think of ideas, rebuild your houses with positive phrases. You might say things such as "I'll try to clean my room without being asked" or "Next time you come home all muddy, I'll listen first to how much fun you had."**

Give families three to five minutes to list positive ideas and to put their houses back together. Invite members of each group to share a moment of prayer together, asking God to help them build each other and their home up through the things they say.

family-friendly Advice

Bring enough film to take pictures of families working together and pictures of their houses. Post the pictures on the church bulletin board. It's a great way to advertise the fun you have on family nights. Attendance will increase if people know they'll get to play with blocks!

To close, visit each table and take a picture of each family and the house that their "love" built.

....

Taking It Home

Have families take the pictures home as refrigerator reminders to build each other up. Encourage families to create their own sets of "building up" blocks on which they write positive words and phrases that will make their home stronger.

....

Bill of Rights

Family Focus: Family members will write lists of personal rights and discover how to humbly give them up to serve others.

Supplies: You'll need Bibles, newsprint, and markers.

Ask members of each family to gather around a table. Invite singles to form small groups of two to four. Give each group a marker and a sheet of newsprint. Explain that the goal of this activity is to create a "bill of rights" for each person present.

To get started, have each family draw lines on the newsprint to create as many sections as there are family members. Then say: **All of us believe that there are certain things we think we should have in life. We feel like we have certain rights. A right is something that we feel we deserve, something that others must give us. Right now, think about what rights you think you should have. For example, you might feel that you have the right to go to bed when you want, the right to be left alone when you want, the right to eat whatever you want, or the right to buy whatever you want. Take a few minutes to think of the rights you believe you should have.**

After several minutes, have family members take turns writing their rights on different sections of the newsprint. Remind parents to help younger children who are unable to write. Allow five to ten minutes for people to list their rights.

When everyone has listed several rights, ask for volunteers to report some of their rights to the rest of the group. After several volunteers have shared, have family members discuss the following questions:

- **What do most of our lists have in common?**
- **How is your list different from other lists?**

Then say: **It's easier to get along as families when we respect each other's rights, but sometimes we need to give up our rights. Let's see what God's Word teaches about when and why we should give up our rights.**

Instruct family members to read aloud Philippians 2:1-8 and then discuss the following questions:

- **What rights do you think Jesus had?**
- **What did Jesus do with his rights?**
- **Why do you think Jesus gave up his rights?**

Allow five minutes for reading and discussion. Then have family groups turn over their sheets of newsprint and list situations in which they should live like Jesus by giving up their rights. For each right listed on the front, have family members brainstorm one situation in which they could show humility by giving up that right.

After groups finish, ask each person to tell the members of his or her family one right he or she will give up in order to show love to a family member during the coming week. Close with a prayer thanking God for Jesus' example of self-sacrificing love and asking God to help each person follow Jesus' example within his or her family.

Taking It Home

Encourage families to take their sheets of newsprint home and to hang them with the "rights" side facing the wall as a symbol of their promise to lay aside their rights to serve others. For extra fun, suggest that family members congratulate each other for doing the "right" thing whenever they see someone willingly giving up a personal right.

All Tied Up

Family Focus: Family members will get "all tied up" to help them understand how sin can snare and entangle them.

Supplies: You'll need Bibles, masking tape, scissors, and a twenty-foot section of soft-woven rope for each group.

Weather permitting, enjoy the first part of this activity outside in an open playing area. Use a large, open room or a gymnasium for this activity if you can't go outside. A fellowship hall will work well if all the tables and chairs are cleared out ahead of time. Use the masking tape to mark a starting line and a finish line.

Have families form their own small groups. Invite people whose families are not present to form small groups of four to five. Give each group a twenty-foot section of rope.

Allow two to three minutes for each group to tie its rope piece around the waists of all the members of the group. (See illustration.) Encourage members to make the rope tight enough to hold them together without slipping off but not so tight as to hurt anyone.

If you're outside, line up all the "tied up" teams and have them race from start to finish. If you're playing inside with limited space, you may want to have teams "run" the course one at a time and time them with a watch. When every group has finished the race, instruct group members to untie themselves and sit down together. Then ask:

- **How did it feel to run a race while tied up?**
- **What would have made the race easier?**

Give each family group a Bible, and ask someone from each group to read aloud Hebrews 12:1. Then have family members discuss the following questions. Ask:

- **What do you think it means for sin to entangle or catch us?**
- **How is being tied up by sin like being tied together with a rope?**
- **In what ways does sin "tie up" the person sinning? others?**

Ask one person from each group to cut the rope into equal-sized lengths, one for each person. When everyone has a piece of rope, say: **Sin often ties us up and keeps us from following God as we should. But sometimes sin causes big problems for others and ties them up, too. Within your family groups, spend a moment thinking of ways sin ties you up. While holding your rope, think about a sin or problem you have that also entangles other family members. You might think of a time you didn't tell the truth and tangled everyone up in your lie. Perhaps you can think of times you became angry and everyone else suffered as a result. Spend a moment thinking and then share your example with your family. When everyone has shared, pray together, asking God for help to stay untied and untangled by sin.**

Allow five minutes for sharing and praying and then close in prayer, asking for God's help to throw off everything that would hinder us from following him. Have families take their rope pieces home as a reminder to stay untangled. To close the meeting, run the race again, this time with family members holding hands as they run. The second race should be a lot faster and more fun than the first.

Taking It Home

Encourage family members to use their rope pieces to create a wall hanging they can use in their home. For example, a family might use the rope pieces for the border around a plaque that has the words to Hebrews 12:1 on it. Challenge families to each keep a piece of rope handy so members can lovingly remind each other of how sin "ties up" both the person sinning and the rest of the family.

Popcorn Love

Family Focus: Family members will enjoy a popcorn party that helps them learn the connection between faith and works.

Supplies: You'll need Bibles, bowls, unpopped popcorn, plenty of freshly popped popcorn, soft drinks, and napkins.

Before the meeting, prepare bowls of unpopped popcorn. You'll need one bowl for each group or family.

To begin, have families form their own small groups. Encourage singles and couples without children to form small groups of four or five. Instruct family members and group members to choose a place to sit together with their families or groups, either at tables or on the floor.

Explain that the meeting's central focus will be a popcorn party for all the families. Ask group members to spend a few minutes naming all the good things about popcorn. Encourage them to be creative. If no one else mentions it, bring up the fact that popcorn can even make a festive (and tasty) Christmas decoration.

When groups have talked about the wonders of popcorn, tell them it's time to enjoy their popcorn party. Then silently give each group a bowl of unpopped popcorn. Encourage family members to enjoy the popcorn as they read James 2:14-17 together. Then ask families to discuss how unpopped popcorn is like and unlike loving words without loving actions.

After several minutes, ask groups to report their ideas. Then have groups describe situations in the family in which love is spoken but not accompanied by action. Allow a few minutes for discussion and then encourage family members each to list one time they haven't backed up loving words with loving actions. Encourage family members to honestly admit and to freely forgive each other for their failures.

When groups finish sharing, bring out freshly popped popcorn for all to enjoy. Set out the drinks, popcorn, bowls, and napkins. While families enjoy the refreshments, ask them to list specific ways to show love to family members through words and actions. Encourage each member of a family or group to select a piece of popcorn for each other member of the group. Ask family members to take turns naming one way they will match loving words with actions for each other group member and then feeding a piece of popcorn to that person. (Suggest that people not in family groups each name two or three significant people in their lives and how they will match loving words with actions for those people.)

Close with several minutes of "popcorn" prayer in which people "pop" up, one at a time, and offer short prayers of thanks to God for families and for his "active" love for them.

Taking It Home

Encourage families to put their loving words into action by having members of each family work together to prepare and deliver a basket of popcorn goodies to a person or family not present at your popcorn party. Be sure families tell their "popcorn pals" that they love them when they deliver the goodies.

Woven Together

Family Focus: Families will learn how emotions can draw them closer to each other and to God.

Supplies: You'll need Bibles and four colors of crepe paper.

Before the meeting, tear the different colors of crepe paper into two-to three-foot lengths. You'll need one strip for each person.

To begin, have families form their own small groups. Invite people whose families are not present to form their own "family" groups of three to five. Give each person a strip of crepe paper. Try to give group members different colors of crepe paper strips.

Have each person think of a time during the past week that a family member made him or her feel happy, angry, loved, sad, or some other emotion. After thirty seconds of "think time," ask family members to take turns using their crepe paper strips to portray those emotions to each other. For example, someone who felt happy might form a huge smile with the crepe paper, while someone who felt angry might wad the paper into a tight ball. Have other group members guess at the emotion being portrayed and then listen attentively as that person explains why he or she felt that emotion.

After five minutes, ask family members to discuss the following questions. Ask:

- **How were our emotions similar? How were they different?**
- **What does this say about the various emotions in our family?**
- **What would it be like if we couldn't feel all these emotions?**
- **How do these emotions draw us closer together? push us apart?**

Then have family members weave or braid their crepe paper strips together. Say: **Sometimes emotions are hard to deal with, but family life would be pretty dull without them. Just as the crepe paper strips can be woven together to create a colorful streamer, our emotions can be woven together to draw us closer as families. God's Word tells us how we can use our emotions to weave ourselves together into close-knit families.**

Ask family members to read Romans 12:15 and then discuss the following questions. After each question, ask for volunteers to report their groups' insights. Ask:

- **Why do you think God wants us to rejoice together? to mourn together?**

- When is it hard to share in other family members' happiness? sadness?
- How can we make it easier to share in each other's happiness? sadness?

Say: **God's Word teaches that sharing and accepting each other's emotions draws us closer together as families. In the same way, honestly sharing our emotions with God draws us closer to him. So let's conclude by telling God what we're feeling right now and by thanking him for accepting us no matter how we feel.**

Ask family members to stand, and have each grasp the family's streamer with one hand. Then have family members take turns telling God how they feel about the family and thanking God for accepting them and their family.

Taking It Home

Suggest that family members make a crepe paper pinwheel to remind them of the importance of respecting each other's emotions. Glue the strips of crepe paper in pinwheel fashion to a sheet of construction paper. Then write various emotions on the crepe paper strips. A family member can point to a strip to "tell" others how he or she is feeling or role play emotions on the pinwheel while others guess what he or she is acting out.

Pick a Pitcher

Family Focus: Family members will "taste" how important it is to tame their tongues.

Supplies: You'll need Bibles, pitchers of water, salt, paper cups, a timer or a watch with a second hand, presweetened drink mixes, a spoon, and snacks.

Prior to this activity, prepare two pitchers of water for each family you expect. Put fresh, cold water in one pitcher and water with at least half a cup of salt in the other. Make sure to stir the salty water well to dissolve all the crystals. Place two prepared pitchers, several paper cups, and a Bible on a table for each group.

Have members of each family gather in a group around a table. Encourage

Family-friendly Advice

Instead of providing two pitchers for each family, you may wish to place six pitchers of water at a central table. Fill three with fresh water and three with saltwater. Invite groups to come to the table and to fill their cups from one of the pitchers.

people whose families are not present to form small groups of four or five and to choose a table. Instruct everyone to take a seat and to wait for instructions before taking a drink.

Say: **Choose a leader from your family or group to pour drinks for everyone at your table. Leaders, pour a drink from whichever pitcher a person prefers. Once everyone has a drink, take a sip and taste the refreshments.**

Wait until everyone has taken a drink. Some will show signs of satisfaction or relief, while others may request a quick drink from the other pitcher. Then ask the entire group:

- **Did you like your drink? Why or why not?**
- **Why did you choose the drink that you did?**
- **What determined the drink you received?**

Say: **The pitchers of water made all the difference. If you chose the saltwater pitcher, you got saltwater. If you chose the fresh-water pitcher, you got fresh water. Whatever was in the pitcher of water determined what you got. Look up James 3:9-12, and read the verses together in your groups.**

Allow families time to read the passage and then ask:

- **In what ways are hurtful words like salty water?**
- **In what ways are helpful words like fresh water?**
- **What do our words reveal about what's inside of us?**

Then explain that you're going to set the timer for three minutes, during which time people are to silently think of times in the past few days when they used "salty" words that hurt other family members. (You may want to allow more time for your group, but younger kids will appreciate three minutes rather than five or more.)

When the timer goes off, encourage family members to take turns holding a cup of saltwater and confessing their hurtful words to one another. After everyone in a group has shared, have family members pray, asking God to help them "refresh" each other with kind words.

While groups are sharing, put the presweetened drink mix in the pitchers of fresh water to create a sweet refreshment. Set out the snacks. Then invite families to enjoy the refreshments as they list all the sweet words they can use to make their home a refreshing place to be.

Taking It Home

Encourage families to spend time in confession with each other on a daily basis. Challenge families to choose a special pitcher for family meals. When water is served from the pitcher, have family members tell of times during the day when they said hurtful or wrong words. Remind families to "confess" the helpful things they said, too!

What Would Love Do?

Family Focus: Families will act out real-life situations and "write in" loving solutions.

Supplies: You'll need Bibles, index cards, and pens or pencils.

Before the meeting, prepare one set of five index cards for each family. Write one situation on each of the five cards. Use five of the following ideas, or write out your own to match the needs of your group:

- You are busy playing, and someone calls your name. What do you do?
- It's the middle of the night, and someone wakes up sick. What would you do?
- New neighbors just moved in and accidentally ran over a bike that you left in the driveway. How do you respond?
- One of your favorite shows is on television when a friend calls. Do you talk or call the friend back?
- You got home late, and you can't wait to fall asleep. Do you pray first or just go right to sleep?
- You have a chance to go to a professional sports event, but you'd miss a special program at church. Which would you choose?
- The house is a mess, and company is due any minute. What would you do?
- You just asked for a cookie and found out that your brother ate the last one. What do you do or say?

Invite families to form small groups. Encourage people whose families are not present to form their own "family" groups of four or five. Hand each group a set of the index-card situations (face down), pens or pencils, and a Bible. Ask people not to read the cards.

Have family members each secretly choose one card and then take turns acting out their situations and how they would react in those situations. Have other group members guess what each situation is and then spend time discussing what they think "love" would do in each circumstance.

After five minutes, ask family members to discuss the following questions. Ask:

- **Which of the situations are like ones that we face at home?**
- **How were our normal responses different from how love would respond? How were they similar?**

Have family members read 1 Corinthians 13:4-5 together. Then have each family member choose a situation card that describes an area of weakness in his or her life. If someone can't find a situation with which he or she struggles, have that person write out his or her own situation on a blank index card. Make sure each person has a card.

Then have family members take turns identifying a portion of the verses that they need to apply to their situations. Encourage family members to work together to write down the sections of the verses they have chosen on the backs of their situation cards.

Say: **God's Word provides a perfect pattern for love. Love isn't easily angered when a new bike gets squashed by a neighbor's car. Love is patient and kind even when someone eats the last homemade chocolate chip cookie. Love isn't rude even when a brother or a sister calls you a name. Love doesn't keep track of how many times your brother hit you yesterday. God's love is a pattern we can follow. We can use these verses as a promise to treat each other with love. So when you encounter different situations like these, you can think of what love would do and then do it.**

Ask family members to put their cards in the center of the group and then hold their hands over the cards. Have family members take turns saying simple prayers promising God and each other that they will try to live as love would in their daily lives.

Taking It Home

Give families blank index cards to take home with them. Encourage families to continue playing What Would Love Do? by writing down situations that actually happen at home and then honestly discussing what happened and what love would do in those situations.

All About Baptism

Family Focus: Families will learn about your church's tradition of baptism.

Supplies Needed: You'll need a church map showing the locations of the learning stations, five to ten colored two-by-four-inch strips of paper for each family, one sheet of colored paper for each family, pencils, and crayons or markers. You'll also need the supplies listed for the learning stations described below.

Before the meeting, set up the following learning stations:

Station 1: When are people baptized? Set out children's Bibles and a fishbowl or a basket containing slips of paper with questions such as "Mom or Dad, when were you baptized?" "Mom or Dad, how were you baptized?" and "Was I baptized as a baby? Why or why not?" on them, one question per slip. Photocopy the following directions, and set the copies at the learning station:

- *Use one of the Bibles to read Acts 16:25–33 together. Then assign each family member a role from this story and act it out. (If there aren't enough people in your family, join another family to act it out.)*
- *Discuss the following questions with your family: What does it mean that the jailer was "saved"? What do you think someone must do to become a Christian? Why do you think the jailer was baptized? Why do you think everyone in the jailer's family was baptized? How can we follow the example of the jailer and his family?*
- *Have each child draw one question from the basket or fishbowl for his or her parent or parents to answer. Return each question when you are done with it.*
- *End in prayer, thanking God for the gift of salvation and for the opportunity to tell others that you are followers of Jesus.*

Station 2: How are people baptized? Locate this station wherever baptism takes place in your church. Arrange for your minister to set out any equipment your church uses for baptism, such as baptismal robes, a handkerchief, or a pitcher. Ask the minister to be prepared to explain to families how people are baptized in your church. Make sure to discuss what people wear, where they get ready, where the water comes from, and so on. Consider arranging for people to touch the water. If there is a choice of baptismal mode in your tradition (sprinkling, pouring, immersion), ask the minister to explain those alternative methods of baptism. If your church requires baptismal candidates to answer questions or recite vows, have the minister explain and give examples of those.

Station 3: Why do we use water? Set out a bar of soap, a pitcher of water, and a container of plant fertilizer. Locate the following stories in children's picture Bibles: Noah and the ark, Moses crossing the Red Sea, Jonah, Jesus' baptism, and Jesus calming the storm. Set out the pictures at the learning station. Photocopy and set out copies of the following directions:

● *Look at the pictures of these Bible stories in which water was important. Tell one another the story behind each picture, and discuss why water was important in that picture. If you'd like, act out one or more of the stories.*

● *Take turns picking up the soap, the fertilizer, and the pitcher of water. Discuss why water is used with each of these things and how those uses remind you of baptism. For example, what does fertilizer do and how might that symbolize baptism? What does soap do? What does a cold pitcher of water do?*

● *End in prayer, thanking God for the gift of water and for using it as a symbol of our commitment to him.*

As families arrive, give them church maps showing where each learning station may be found. Explain that family members will go through three learning stations together to discover when, how, and why people are baptized. Families may spend up to fifteen minutes at each station and then move on to a new station. Ask families to return to your meeting area in forty-five minutes even if they have not finished every station. Then encourage family groups to scatter among the stations so no station becomes overly crowded.

Circulate among the stations, and remind people to move on every fifteen minutes. When forty-five minutes is up, encourage families to return to your meeting area.

When everyone has returned, have each family form a group. Give each family five to ten strips of colored paper, one sheet of colored paper, a pencil, and several crayons or markers.

Encourage children to write on each strip one thing they learned about baptism or one question they still have about baptism. Remind parents to help younger children who cannot write well. While kids are working, parents are to write a baptismal prayer for their kids on the sheet of paper. The prayer can offer thanks that a child has already been baptized or ask God to encourage a child to be baptized at the right time. Families with several children may need to include both of these options.

After several minutes, have children share with their parents all the things they learned about baptism and present the question slips to the parents. Then ask parents to read their baptismal prayers to their children as a concluding prayer.

....

Taking It Home

Encourage families to continue learning and talking about baptism at home. Parents can take time to answer any questions their kids still have about baptism. Kids will enjoy decorating, framing, and hanging their special baptismal prayers.

....

Worship Experiences

Shining Lights

Family Focus: Families will talk about the purpose of worship and create special candles for their home worship areas.

Supplies: You will need Bibles, eight-by-seventeen-inch sheets of colored beeswax, wicks, small clay pots, scissors or knives, a small garden trowel, a bag of sand, and books of matches.

Family-Friendly Advice
You can usually find beeswax at craft stores. If a craft store near you doesn't carry beeswax, ask for the name and phone number of a supplier.

Before the meeting, set out the materials on tables around the room. If you'd like, play worship music quietly in the background.

As people arrive, invite them to form family groups. Those who are not with their families should be invited to form groups of four to six. Then lead everyone in several praise or worship songs that kids and adults are likely to know.

After two or three songs, say: **We have gathered together as God's family to worship God. Worshiping together strengthens and encourages us. But worship isn't reserved for Sunday morning or when we come to church. We can worship as families any time and any place. We've started with singing, which is something we often do in worship. Within your small group, talk about other things that we include in our worship services.**

Allow several minutes for discussion and then call the groups back to attention and ask kids and adults to share what they talked about. As people respond, particularly highlight prayer, reading God's Word, and teaching. Then say: **We are going to spend some time now reading the Bible. In your groups, please read Matthew 5:14-16; Luke 11:33-36; and John 1:1-8.** Allow time for the groups to read the passages. Then ask:

- What common theme did you notice in these passages?
- Why do you think light is an important biblical symbol?

Say: **When we worship in church, we often light candles to remind us that Jesus is the light and that those who know him can shine his light in the world. On the tables you will find sheets of beeswax and wicks. Let's take some time for everyone to create a candle as a reminder of Jesus, the Light of the World.**

Explain how to make a simple candle (for younger children) and a more complex candle (for older kids and adults). To make a simple candle, cut a rectangular strip of beeswax three to four inches wide and eight inches long. Lay a wick along one edge and then roll the wax tightly around the wick. (Encourage parents to help younger kids make their candles.) This easy method requires no heat at all!

To make a complex candle, cut a sheet of beeswax diagonally, lay a thin strip of another color of beeswax along the angled edge (overlapping the edges slightly), lay a wick along the short edge, and roll the wax toward the opposite point of the angled edge. (See illustration.)

Once everyone has completed a candle, say: **Gather in your groups, and take a moment to thank God for sending Jesus to be the light of the world.** Allow time for prayer and then sing "This Little Light of Mine" together.

Then say: **Turn now in your Bibles to 2 Corinthians 4:5-7, and read those verses together in your groups.** Allow time for groups to read. Then say: **God's light shines in us even though we are not perfect. So we can worship God because we know that God has made us his own through Jesus Christ. As a reminder that God's light shines in jars of clay, take a**

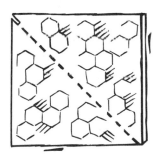 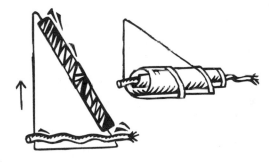

clay pot and use the garden trowel to fill your family's pot about half full of sand. Then set one of your family's candles solidly into the sand.

Allow time for families to set their candles and then say: **Gather your family in a circle and, beginning with the person whose candle is in the pot, take turns sharing with your family members one way you can shine God's light in your family.**

After several minutes, say: **I would like an adult from your group to come forward and get a book of matches from me. When you return to your group, light the candle in your clay pot. Then I will say a prayer, and we will conclude our worship with a song.** When all the candles are lit, say a prayer thanking God for sending Jesus as the light and for sending us into the world as his lights. Close with an appropriate song, such as "Walkin' in the Light" or "This Little Light of Mine."

Taking It Home

Encourage families to take their candles home and to put them in a special family worship area. Remind families to light their candles as a reminder that Jesus' light shines in their families whenever they gather to read God's Word or to have family devotions.

Family Communion Workshop

Family Focus: Family members will explore the story of Jesus' Last Supper and your church's tradition of the Lord's Table.

Supplies: You'll need church maps showing where the learning stations are located, poster board, construction paper, scissors, glue, markers or crayons, and tape. You'll also need the supplies listed for each of the three learning stations described below.

Before the meeting, set up the following learning stations. Allow enough resources at each learning station so several families can be there at the same time:

● **Station 1: The Last Supper.** Set out several children's Bibles, markers, and sheets of tan paper cut into the shape of bread loaves. Write the following instructions on a sheet of newsprint, and hang it at the learning station:

Read about Jesus' Last Supper in Matthew 26:17-30; Mark 14:12-26; or Luke

22:7-20. Discuss as a family the following questions. Write your answers on a sheet of loaf-shaped paper:

Who was there?

What did they eat?

What did Jesus say and do?

When we share the Lord's Table, we remember Jesus and his Last Supper. What about this would make us sad? happy?

- **Station 2: The Lord's Table.** Arrange for a minister to display all the items your church uses to prepare and to serve the Lord's Table. If possible, locate this station at your Communion table and set out several types of bread, the equipment used to fill the Communion cups, and several Communion cups. Photocopy the box containing the words of institution (see page 30), one copy for each family. Ask the minister to explain to participants who may take Communion in your church, how often it is offered, and your church practices involving how one receives the elements. Remind the minister to give each family a copy of the words of institution.

- **Station 3: We Remember.** Set out a collection of mementos such as vacation photos, seashells, and baby shoes. Also post storybook pictures from the life of Jesus around the station. Then write the following instructions on a sheet of newsprint, and hang it at the station:

Look at the souvenirs and mementos on the table. Talk about what each one would help someone remember. Then take turns sharing stories of your favorite family memories.

Look at the pictures of Jesus. Discuss what you remember about the stories behind these pictures. Then think of ways that you as a family can remember Jesus during your daily lives.

As families arrive, give them church maps showing where each learning station may be found. Explain that family members will go through three learning stations together to explore the Last Supper and your church's tradition regarding the Lord's Table. Families may spend up to fifteen minutes at each station and then move on to a new station. Ask families to return to your meeting area in forty-five minutes even if they have not finished every station. Then ask family groups to scatter among the stations so no station gets overly crowded.

Circulate among the stations, and remind people to move to new stations every fifteen minutes. When forty-five minutes is up, encourage families to return to your meeting area.

When everyone has returned, have each family form a group. Point out the poster board, construction paper, scissors, glue, tape, and markers or crayons. Instruct each family to create a colorful poster that shows what family members learned about the Last Supper and the Lord's Table.

Allow families five to ten minutes to create their posters and then invite each family to show and explain its poster to the rest of the group. After every family has shared, sing a song together such as "Let Us Break Bread Together." Then close in prayer, thanking God for the gift of his Son and for this way to remember him.

Taking It Home

Suggest that families set aside one meal a week to recall a story from Jesus' life. For example, families might serve fish and chips and talk about the feeding of the five thousand. For more fun food ideas, see Incredible Edible Bible Fun *by Nanette Goings (Group Publishing, 1997).*

Words of Institution

Read the following responsively, with parents taking Part 1 and kids reading Part 2.

Part 1: What happened at Jesus' Last Supper with his disciples?

Part 2: The Lord Jesus, on the night of his arrest, took bread and, after giving thanks to God, broke it.

Part 1: How was that different from all the other times Jesus had broken bread with his disciples?

Part 2: This time he said, "This is my body, which is for you; this do, remembering me."

Part 1: And then what happened?

Part 2: In the same way, he took the cup after supper.

Part 1: How was that different from all the other times Jesus had shared a cup with his disciples?

Part 2: He said: "This cup is the new covenant sealed in my blood. Whenever you drink it, do this, remembering me."

Part 1: Then why are we eating this bread and drinking from this cup today?

Part 2: Because every time we eat this bread and drink from this cup, we proclaim the death of the Lord until he comes.

The Breath of Prayer

Family Focus: Family members will discover how they can worship God together through prayer.

Supplies: You'll need Bibles, one uninflated balloon for each person, one helium-filled balloon for each family or person whose family is not present, photocopies of the card on page 32, and tape.

Before the meeting, make photocopies of the card on page 32. Tape one copy to each helium-filled balloon.

As families arrive, ask them to sit together in groups. Encourage those whose families aren't present to form groups of four to five. Give each group a Bible, and give each person an uninflated balloon.

Say: **Today we want to worship God through prayer—but not just prayer in general. We want to worship God through family prayer, by praying as Jesus taught us in the Bible. It is appropriate, then, that we begin with a prayer.** Offer a short opening prayer.

Instruct group members to read together Luke 11:1-13 and then discuss the following questions:

- **What things can we say to God in prayer?**
- **What gives us confidence when we pray?**
- **What can we ask God for when we pray?**

After several minutes of discussion, ask for volunteers to report their groups' insights about prayer. Then say, **When we began, I gave each of you a balloon. We are going to use these balloons to teach us about prayer. But first I'd like you to take another look at Luke 11:2-4. These verses record the Lord's Prayer, which gives us a wonderful outline for how we should pray. As a group, talk about what types of things we should pray about based on the Lord's Prayer. Then, after a few minutes, I will direct you to begin your own prayers.**

Allow time for discussion and then say: **We're now ready to begin our prayers. However, we are going to do something special as we pray. I'd like the oldest person in your group to say a short prayer. Then, when that person is done praying, each person in your group should blow a puff of**

Family-Friendly Advice

You may want to suggest that parents of younger children blow the puff of air into the balloon for them. That will help avoid letting the air out of the balloon.

air into his or her balloon and squeeze the end shut. Then someone else in your group is to say a short prayer, and you'll all blow into your balloons again. Continue this way until everyone has prayed. Use the Lord's Prayer as a guide for what to pray about. Please begin your prayers.

Allow adequate time for prayer. You may even may wish to play music quietly in the background as groups pray. When everyone has finished praying, ask the younger children in the group:

● What would happen if we let go of all these balloons?

● Where do you think our prayers go when we say them?

● How is letting a balloon go like sending a prayer to God?

Then explain that you are going to close with a short prayer, after which each person should release the breath of the prayer without letting go of the balloon. Pray: **Lord, we are thankful for your great love for us. You have made it possible for us to speak to you at any time. Thank you for your Son Jesus, who has taught us that we can come to you as children come to a father. Our lives are lifted to you this day as we release the breath of our prayers. Amen.** Have people release the air from their balloons.

As everyone leaves, give each family, single, and couple a helium balloon with a card from this page attached.

This balloon is a reminder that every time you pray, your words rise to God. He hears your prayers and responds in love. Your family will be strengthened whenever you worship God together in prayer.

Taking It Home

Suggest that families use markers to write their prayers on inflated balloons. The balloons will remind families to pray regularly. When God answers a prayer, families can carefully deflate the balloon and glue it to a colorful "prayer poster," which will remind them of all the prayers God has answered for them.

Bible Presentation

Family Focus: Parents will present Bibles to their kids and commit to read the Bible regularly with their kids.

Supplies: You'll need age-appropriate Bibles, one for each child or teenager you expect.

This activity works well as part of a regular worship service. Decide which age of children you want to present with Bibles, and purchase appropriate Bibles for that age of child. Bible storybooks are loved by kindergartners, while children's Bibles work well for second-graders. If you're going to present Bibles to kids entering junior high, challenge parents to purchase age-appropriate study Bibles for their kids.

Begin the service with a short children's sermon or devotional focusing on the importance of God's Word and on parents' need to teach their kids about God's Word. You may want to use 2 Timothy 3:16-17 and Deuteronomy 6:4-9 as your key Scriptures.

If kids are already sitting up front for the children's message, call the parents forward and have them stand with their children. Otherwise, invite parents and kids to come forward and stand together.

If you're presenting Bible storybooks, have volunteers give one Bible storybook to each kindergartner. For second-graders, ask the volunteers to distribute children's Bibles to the parents. Remind parents of junior high kids to bring the study Bibles when they come forward.

Say: **One way parents can keep their commitment to train their children well is by reading the Bible with them on a regular basis. When you as parents read the Bible to and with your kids, you help them learn to love and follow God more powerfully than anyone in the church could ever do.**

Then instruct people to present their Bibles—kindergartners to their parents and parents of second-graders and junior-highers to their kids—and have parents promise to read the Bible to and with their kids on a regular basis.

When the Bibles have been presented, close in prayer, asking God to help parents keep their promises and to honor those commitments by creating in parents and children alike a love for God and for his Word.

Taking It Home

To encourage parents and kids to read the Bible together often, give each family a special bookmark to put in the Bible. For example, you might present second-graders and junior-highers each a bookmark with a Bible reading plan on it. Parents of kindergartners, however, would probably appreciate a bookmark that explains how to read Bible stories in a fun and interesting way.

This activity adapted from an activity described by Ben Freudenburg in Family Ministry: How Your Church Can Strengthen the Home *by Ben Freudenburg and Rick Lawrence (Group Publishing, 1998).*

Family Passover

family focus: Families will explore the Passover story and the symbolic foods of a Passover dinner.

Supplies: You'll need children's Bibles, baking powder, baking soda, yeast, regular bread, one sheet of matzo per family (available in most larger grocery stores), paper lunch-bags, matches, bowls of saltwater, plastic spoons, parsley, horseradish, apples, cinnamon, walnuts (optional), grape juice, knives, a cutting board, and mixing bowls. (If you have any difficulty locating Passover resources, check with your local Christian bookstore or food stores specializing in Jewish food products.)

family-friendly Advice

One purpose of Passover is for parents to teach their children, but a long, formal Passover dinner can be less than instructional for many younger children. If your church has a Passover celebration, use this activity to prepare families for the actual Passover dinner. You may also want to hold this activity instead of a formal Passover dinner and conclude it with an informal dinner.

Before the meeting, prepare one table for each family you expect. Set the following items on each table: a children's Bible, a piece of regular bread, a sheet of matzo, a paper lunch-bag, a bowl of saltwater, several plastic spoons, several sprigs of parsley, and a small dish of horseradish. Then hide pieces of regular bread around a room close to your meeting room.

As each family arrives, ask family members to sit together at a table. When everyone has arrived, briefly explain the background of Passover. Be sure to mention the Israelite slavery in Egypt and God's use of plagues to convince Pharaoh to let the Israelites go. Challenge the entire group to name as many of the plagues as they can recall. Suggest that people look up Exodus 7:14–10:29 to find the first nine plagues.

Then say: **In spite of all these signs, Pharaoh still refused to let God's people go. So God sent one final, horrible plague to convince Pharaoh to free the Israelites. As a family, read together about this final plague in Exodus 11:4-8 and 12:3-13, 28-32.**

Allow several minutes for reading and then ask family members to discuss the following questions:

- **What was the final plague that God sent on the Egyptians?**
- **Why do you think God had the Israelites sacrifice a lamb?**
- **Why do you think people remember this as "the Passover"?**

Then say: **Since that first night, Jewish people have remembered**

God's deliverance and protection by celebrating the Passover once a year. During this celebration, people remember certain details about God's protection of them.

Hold up the containers of baking powder, baking soda, and yeast. Explain that all these things contain "leaven," which makes bread, cake, or cookies rise and look puffy. Then have families look at the two pieces of bread on the table and decide which one has leaven in it. Encourage everyone to taste a piece of matzo. Then have families read together Exodus 12:37-39 to learn the meaning of the matzo.

Say: **God told the Jewish people to eat no leaven during Passover, so they remove it from their houses before Passover begins.** Lead the group into the room where you have hidden pieces of bread. Instruct families to hunt for the bread, put it in a paper bag, and then burn it out of doors or in a church fireplace to get rid of it.

When all the bread is gone, have families return to their tables. Then say: **During the Passover, there is a time for children to ask, "Why is tonight different from all other nights?" What do we know already that is different about a Passover meal?**

Allow time for responses and then explain that Passover dinners are also different from regular meals in other ways. Ask each person to dip a spoon into the bowl of saltwater and taste it. Then ask:

- **What did you taste in the water?**
- **What other times have you tasted saltwater?**

Then explain that life was so hard for the Jewish slaves that they often cried. The Passover saltwater reminds people of the tears shed in Egypt. But God also parted the Red Sea after the people were free, so the saltwater reminds people of the way God delivered his people from Egypt. Then explain that people usually taste the saltwater by dipping a sprig of parsley into it. After each person does this, have families list all the ways tonight (Passover night) is different from all other nights.

Then say: **The Passover dinner also includes vegetables, of course. But we eat special vegetables. To remember that life as a slave was bitter, we eat a vegetable that is very bitter.** Encourage everyone to take a small taste of horseradish and then list all the ways tonight is different from all other nights.

Say: **The Bible tells us that the Jewish slaves worked in Egypt to build the pyramids and palaces for the Pharaoh and his officials. For Passover, we make a special food that reminds us of the mortar the slaves used to hold the bricks together in their building.** So children can see that the contents of this food are familiar and "safe," chop up an apple, add a bit of cinnamon and some ground walnuts (optional), and then moisten it all with grape juice. Offer each person a taste of the mixture, which is called *charoset*. Have everyone make a sandwich out of two pieces of matzo, *charoset*, and a tiny bit of horseradish. Then ask: **Who can remember what each food stands for?**

Allow time for responses and then say: **During the time of Jesus, the people also ate roasted lamb as the meat for their Passover dinner. In the New Testament, Jesus is referred to as the Lamb of God.** Ask:

- **Why was the lamb important at the very first Passover?**
- **In what ways is Jesus like the lamb killed at Passover?**
- **What are some ways we can remember Jesus' death for us?**

If you would like, conclude this activity with a family Communion in which you use matzo for bread. Remind people of the parallels between the unleavened matzo and the sinless body of Jesus, which the matzo represents. Conclude your service with a hymn, just as Jesus and the disciples did at Jesus' last Passover (Matthew 26:30).

If you prefer, adjourn to a simple dinner at which you serve the Passover foods, including roast lamb. Some congregations end the Passover celebration with round dancing from Israel. So consider praising God through dance! Check out a folk dance record from the library, or call a local Jewish synagogue to hire a dance teacher.

Taking It Home

Encourage each family to celebrate Passover together in the home—just as it was originally intended. The script for a Passover meal is called the Haggadah. You can find a Messianic Haggadah in many Christian bookstores.

Mezuza Messages

family Focus: Family members will make a mezuza (Scripture box) and discover how to worship God by learning his Word.

Supplies: You'll need Bibles, construction paper, scissors, glue, tape, markers or crayons, ribbon, index cards, pencils, and one small shoe box for each family, single, or couple.

Before the meeting, set out the supplies. As families arrive, ask them to form family groups. Encourage singles and couples without children to join family groups or to form their own small groups.

To begin, ask someone to read aloud Deuteronomy 6:4-9. Then ask someone else to read verses 6-9 again. Explain that the people of ancient Israel obeyed this command in several ways. For example, the Israelites tied small boxes (called phylacteries) that contained Bible verses on their wrists and foreheads whenever they prayed. In addition, Israelite families fastened small boxes (called mezuzas) containing Bible verses on the doorframes of their houses.

Then ask the entire group:

- **Why do you think the Israelites put mezuzas on their houses?**
- **Why do you think it's important to remember God? God's Word?**
- **How does remembering God's Word help us worship God?**

Then say: **One way to worship God is by remembering and obeying his Word. So let's spend a few minutes making mezuzas that we can take home as a reminder that we can worship God by honoring God's Word.**

Point out the shoe boxes and the other supplies. Then invite each family, single, or couple to select a shoe box and various supplies to decorate a box. Encourage group members to discuss how they want to decorate their box and then to all work together to make it look distinctively their own. Explain, however, that each group will need to cut a slit in the lid of its box and leave room to write on both sides of the slit.

Allow families ten minutes to work on their creations and then ask each group to write the following sentence on its box lid: "Your Word we have hidden in our hearts...and placed in our home!" Then give each family twelve index cards, a pencil, and a Bible. Invite family members to write on each card the words to one Bible verse that they would like to learn and remember.

When all the cards are done, have family members slip the cards through the slits in their boxes and then thank God for the gift of his Word. Encourage families to take home their boxes and to work together to learn and apply one verse each month.

Taking It Home

Suggest that each family keep its mezuza in a prominent spot in the house. This will remind family members to worship God by honoring and obeying his Word. It may also provide opportunities to tell visitors what a mezuza is and to explain why the family has one in the house.

Honor to Whom It Is Due

family focus: Family members will create "honor rolls" for God and for their parents.

Supplies: You'll need Bibles, 8½-by-11-inch sheets of parchment paper, pencils, markers, six-inch lengths of ribbon, and self-adhesive stickers in the shapes of stars, hearts, and sunbursts.

Have members of each family sit together in a group. Then ask the entire group the following questions:

- What does it mean to "honor" someone?
- What are ways we honor others? God?
- Why is it important to honor other people?
- Why is it important to give honor to God?

Say: **One way we honor others is by giving them special papers or certificates that tell why they are so important. We can do the same thing for God. So let's create "honor rolls" that tell God exactly why we love and worship him.**

Invite each family to take a sheet of parchment and materials to decorate it. Have family members discuss what specific thing they would like to worship God for and then create a certificate honoring God for that thing. Encourage families to make their certificates fun and official-looking.

After five to ten minutes, have families take turns displaying and explaining their honor rolls to the rest of the group. Then have each family roll up the parchment, tie a ribbon around the honor roll, and then "present" it to God in a family prayer.

family-friendly Advice

Be especially sensitive to the different family situations that may be represented in the room. Some adults may have lost their parents; some children may be from single-parent or blended families. Offer the option of creating a certificate for only one parent or for stepparents.

When everyone is finished, have family groups read Exodus 20:12 and then answer the following questions:

- Why do you think God wants us to honor our parents?
- What are different ways we can honor our parents?

Then say: **Honoring our parents isn't something we should do just when we're younger. God wants us to honor our parents no matter how young or how old we might be. So let's all make honor rolls that tell why our parents are**

so important to us.

Explain that each parent is to create an honor roll for his or her parents and that the children in each family are to work together to make an honor roll for their parents. Remind participants to create certificates that tell why their parents are so special.

After five to ten minutes, have parents show their children what they created. Then invite kids to present their "tied-up" honor rolls to their parents. To close, have family members pray together, individually thanking God for their parents and asking God to help them give honor to God and to their parents.

Taking It Home

Suggest that families laminate their certificates and then either hang them somewhere in the home or present them to grandparents. What a wonderful gift to present to Grandma and Grandpa on their next visit!

Significant Symbols of God

Family Focus: Family members will discover how concrete symbols can help them worship God in spirit.

Supplies: You'll need Bibles, sheets of paper, pencils, a rock, and a flashlight or a lantern.

To begin, have each family form a small group. Encourage people whose families are not there to join a family group or to form their own small groups of four or five.

Give each group a sheet of paper and a pencil. Then say: **One of the things we do when we come to church is worship God.** Ask:

 • **What are some of the ways we worship God at church?**

Encourage children and adults to call out their answers. After a number of responses, challenge each group to write on its sheet of paper a simple and clear definition of worship. The only rule is that everyone in the group must understand the definition.

After several minutes, ask for volunteers to report their groups' definitions. When everyone who wants to has reported, say: **Now we know what wor-**

ship is, so we're ready to discover what God's Word teaches about *how* we should worship God.

Ask group members to read John 4:24 together and then discuss the following questions:

- **What do you think it means to worship God in spirit?**
- **What do you think it means to worship God in truth?**

Say: **We can worship God in spirit by talking to God in prayer. We can worship God in truth by telling God exactly how we feel and by praising him for who he really is. Of course, since God is Spirit, sometimes it's hard to understand who God is or what he is really like. That's why the Bible uses symbols to help us understand and worship God for who he is.**

Hold up the rock, and ask for a volunteer to read aloud Psalm 95:1. Then ask the entire group the following questions:

- **What characteristics of a rock are also true of God?**
- **In what ways do you think God is a rock to his people?**
- **In what specific ways has God been a rock in your life?**

Then invite members of each group to pray together for thirty seconds, thanking God for being a rock in their lives.

After thirty seconds, say "amen." Then hold up the flashlight or lantern, and have a volunteer read aloud Psalm 18:28. Ask the entire group the previous three questions, substituting the word "light" for "rock." Give families thirty seconds to thank God together for being a light in their lives.

After thirty seconds, say "amen." Then invite family members to go on a walk outside or around the church to discover other symbols that help them understand and worship God. Tell families that they have fifteen minutes to find and retrieve at least one item that they can show and explain to the rest of the group. Remind families to be back in fifteen minutes.

When everyone returns, invite each family to show its item and to explain how that item helps family members understand and worship God. When each group has presented its symbol, say: **One look around this room reveals that God has given us many reasons and ways to worship him. So let's close by worshiping God in a prayer of thanks for all God has done for us.** Ask all the members of each family to put their hands on the family's symbolic item and then lead the group in a closing prayer.

Taking It Home

Encourage families to take home their significant symbols and to put them in a special worship area in their homes. Challenge families to add other symbols that they find on walks outside, on family vacations, or even around the house.

As for Me and My House

family focus: Family members will learn how they can "pass" the baton of faith to each other and to others.

Supplies: You'll need Bibles, cardboard paper-towel tubes, markers, construction paper, scissors, transparent tape, and decorative ribbon.

Before the meeting, set out the cardboard paper-towel tubes (one per family) and the decorating supplies.

Begin by asking how many children and adults have ever run in a race. Ask several volunteers to tell the entire group stories of their races. Then ask someone who has competed in a relay race to explain (or demonstrate) how a relay is different from a regular race. Make sure to mention that dropping a baton means disqualification.

Say: **The most crucial part of a relay is the baton pass. It doesn't matter how fast a relay team runs if they can't pass the baton well. One drop of the baton and they're out of the race. It's the same way with our families. Parents may do all sorts of things really well, but if they don't pass the "baton of faith" to their kids, they really haven't succeeded. So let's learn a little more about passing the baton from one person to another.**

Have each family select a paper-towel tube and then decorate the tube so it's distinctively their own. Families might write their last names on the tubes or add designs that represent their families.

After five to ten minutes, invite families to compete in some fun relays. Have family members practice passing their baton and then race in hopping, skipping, running, obstacle course, and backward-walking relays. Give each family a round of applause for its efforts.

Then have family members discuss the following questions:
- **What was hardest about passing the baton? about receiving it?**
- **How is this like passing the baton of faith? How is it different?**
- **What would make it easier to successfully pass along our faith?**

Direct family groups to read Ephesians 6:1-4 and then discuss the following questions:
- **What is parents' responsibility in passing on faith? kids'?**
- **Kids, what good things have your parents passed on to you?**
- **Parents, how have your kids taken the baton of faith from you?**
- **What can you do to pass or receive the baton of faith better?**

Ask for a volunteer to read aloud Joshua 24:15. Then say: **To pass on the baton of faith successfully, each family member needs to be committed to passing or receiving it. So let's conclude our time by having each family member commit to doing his or her part to pass the baton of faith in your family.**

Have family members each grasp the family baton. Then encourage family groups to close in prayer, thanking God for the gift of family and committing themselves to passing on the baton of faith within their family. While family members are still grasping the baton, ask everyone to repeat together: **As for me and my family, we will serve the Lord!**

Taking It Home

Have families take their batons home. Then, whenever one person is doing something positive to "pass on the faith," have another family member hand that person the baton. Also, if family members leave one end of their baton open, they can pass encouraging notes or Scripture verses to each other in the baton.

Las Posadas

Family Focus: Families will role play Mary and Joseph's attempt to find a place for Jesus to be born.

Supplies: You'll need church maps that designate the rooms families will visit and a manger.

In Mexico, the Las Posadas tradition finds children dressed as Mary and Joseph trekking with their families from house to house seeking a "room in the inn" for Jesus to be born. They are turned away, time and again, until they arrive at a designated house that agrees to provide shelter and a place for families and friends to gather for a celebration. This is an adaptation of Las Posadas to fit your church facility.

Before the meeting, choose six to twelve rooms families can visit as they search for a room in the inn. Mark each room on a church map and then make one photocopy of the map for each family. Be sure to note which room families are to visit last. Place the manger in the last room, making sure this room is large enough for everyone to gather in. (If you'd like, decorate the rooms to look like "houses" in Jesus' day.) Arrange for an "innkeeper" to monitor each room. Explain that all the innkeepers except the one in the last room are to refuse shelter to Mary and Joseph. The innkeeper in the final room should tell Mary and Joseph: "I can find you a place to stay in my stable. Your baby can be born there." Ask each family to bring simple head coverings and costumes for one Mary and one Joseph.

When families arrive, ask each family to designate one child to act as Mary and one as Joseph. Explain that other family members will "travel" with Mary and Joseph as they search for a room in the inn where Jesus can be born. Have Mary and Joseph put on their head coverings and costumes.

Give each family a map of "Bethlehem" (the church facility). Then explain that families are to travel together to the various locations on the map. Families can begin at any point and proceed in any order, but they need to visit the designated "inn" last. Each time a family approaches an inn, Joseph is to say: "My wife, Mary, is going to have a baby. Can we stay here for the baby to be born?" Mary, Joseph, and their traveling companions are to keep seeking shelter until they can find it.

When every family has visited every spot and finally been allowed to enter the final room (the stable), have family groups sit together on the floor. Then have your designated worship leader begin singing in a worshipful manner the chorus to "O, Come All Ye Faithful." Sing through the chorus several times. Then invite members of each family to pray together, thanking Jesus for being born and inviting him to "stay" in their family. Close by singing Christmas songs such as "Away in a Manger" or "Silent Night."

Taking It Home

Encourage families to buy or make their own Nativity scenes. Then challenge members of each family to gather around their Nativity scene and discuss ways they might make Jesus unwelcome in their home and ways they can make Jesus "more at home" all year long.

Service Projects

Home-Based Service

family focus: Family members will work together to make a pizza and learn how to serve others as a family.

Supplies: You'll need Bibles, index cards, pens or pencils, and pizza ingredients. To simplify preparations, ask each family attending to bring a different pizza ingredient.

This activity is a fun and effective way to introduce families to the concept of home-based service. You may want to hold this event before you implement the rest of the ideas in this chapter.

Several weeks prior to this event, ask a family that has already completed a service project together if they would agree to share their story with other families. The story should tell people what was involved in the project, obstacles that needed to be overcome, and the benefits (both to the ones being served and to the family) that resulted from their service.

When it's time for this event, have parents and kids gather at the church to make pizzas. Set out the ingredients, but make sure members of each family work together to make their own pizza. Encourage family members to volunteer for different roles, such as Dough-Stretcher, Cheese-Grater, Sauce-Spreader, and Topping-Placer.

While the pizzas are baking, have the family you recruited share their service story. This will give other families a vision for home-based service. Encourage listeners to ask lots of questions so they can get a clear idea of how each family member helped and how the entire family benefited from the experience.

Thank the family for sharing its story and then pray for and enjoy your meal—with family members sitting together. After five to ten minutes, ask family members to read Galatians 6:9-10 and then discuss the following questions:

- **What were the benefits of working together to make a pizza?**
- **Why do you think God wants us to serve one another? others?**
- **What are some different ways we could serve each other? others?**
- **How might serving someone outside the family benefit them? How might it benefit us?**

Ask for volunteers to share their families' ideas for ways they could serve others. Write each idea on an index card. If necessary, supplement people's suggestions with some of the ideas from later in this chapter or with these ideas.

- At home: clean one room, rake leaves, wash windows, or clean gutters.
- At church: clean pews, rake leaves, or fold bulletins.
- In the community: adopt a nursing home resident, work for an elderly neighbor, or volunteer at a homeless shelter or food bank.

After you've listed about five more ideas than there are families attending, spread the index cards out on a table. Then invite family members to look over the different ideas and to take one that their family will agree to perform.

After every family has selected a service idea, challenge family members to decide specifically how and for whom they will perform the service. Encourage each family to write the details of its service project on the back of the index card. After several minutes, close with a prayer dedicating families and their efforts to God.

To send people off in a serving mood, challenge families to serve each other by cleaning up leftover pizza ingredients and washing the dishes.

family-friendly Advice

To remind families to follow through with their commitments, set a pizza-party date two or three months from now. Families can gather to tell about their service projects. Ask everyone to bring videos or photographs of their family in action!

Taking It Home

Suggest that members of each family plan a special pizza party to celebrate the completion of their service project. Encourage family members to list the benefits their service produced—both for them and for the people they served. Challenge families to decide how to keep serving others, whether by choosing new service projects or by continuing the service projects they already started.

This activity adapted from the "home-style service project" described in Ben Freudenburg's article, "Family-Building Events," GROUP Magazine (January/February 1997).

Secret Service

Family Focus: Family members will work together to plan secret ways to serve others.

Supplies: You'll need Bibles, index cards, newsprint, and a marker.

Before the meeting, prepare a set of index cards for each family group. Write one of the following phrases on each card:

- Shake your head when you answer.
- Smile constantly.
- Scratch your nose.
- Cross your legs.
- Fold your arms across your chest.
- Yawn when you answer.
- Tap your fingers on the table.

Ask families to form their own small groups and to gather around tables. Invite those whose family members are not present to form groups of four to six.

Explain that, during the first part of the meeting, everyone will be playing a game of Secret Agent. Everyone is to try to discover which secret actions are being performed by other family members. The only way to complete the mission is for family members to ask each other various questions and then observe how the person answering acts when he or she responds. Encourage people to ask fun questions concerning things they always wanted to know about each other.

If everyone understands the rules, instruct family members to each choose a prepared index card from the pile in the center of the tables, making sure that no one sees the card. Have people read and follow the instructions as family members take turns interrogating each other. Challenge groups to try to discover the secret action of each person. When a person's secret action is discovered, begin questioning the person to his or her right.

Give families five minutes to try to solve the secret actions. Then explain that it was obvious in some situations what was being done. But it took time to figure out some secrets. Maybe some were never uncovered! Ask families to read Matthew 6:1-4 and 25:34-40 together and then discuss why we should serve secretly and what might happen if we didn't serve in secret.

While people are discussing, hang a sheet of newsprint on which to

record people's ideas. After several minutes, ask the entire group to name people they could serve without being discovered. Shut-ins, prisoners, needy families, service organizations, local shelters, and church members who need extra
help are all good possibilities. Write people's ideas on the newsprint. Then have
people list possible ways to serve each group. Write the ideas on the newsprint.

When you have filled the newsprint with service ideas, ask each family to
adopt one group or person who needs help. Then encourage each family to
plan a "secret service" to meet that need. Let families decide what specifically
to do, but offer examples of service, such as collecting canned goods or used
items at home and donating them to a local rescue mission.

If a needy person has been selected, try to determine what needs are represented and how to fill those needs anonymously. Financial support is often
needed. Pay off a doctor bill anonymously. That will leave the recipient guess-
ing and thankful! Allow each member of the family to contribute ideas as well
as actual service. To close, have families pray for their chosen secret service,
asking God to bless it and help it to remain a secret.

Taking It Home

*Take Secret Service home by encouraging everyone in the family to select
one person to serve during the next week. Suggest simple surprise services such
as cleaning up without being asked, picking flowers, or leaving gifts of candy or
treats on someone's pillow. To ensure that everyone gets served, put names in a
hat and draw each Monday morning to see who will serve whom.*

Family Coupons

Family Focus: Families will each team up with another family and find ways to creatively serve one another.

Supplies: You'll need index cards, pens, markers, and staplers.

P lace index cards, pens, markers, and staplers on tables, one table for
each family or small group.
As people arrive, ask members of each family to sit together at a table.
Singles can form their own small groups and sit together. When everyone has

arrived, ask each group to pair up with another group they know well or with whom they have something in common. Suggest that families with small children team up and that singles' groups team up with other singles' groups. If there are an uneven number of groups, have three families form a service triangle, with Family A serving Family B, Family B serving Family C, and Family C serving Family A.

When every family has been teamed up, invite children and adults in both families to discuss different daily struggles or chores they face. For example, people might mention things such as laundry, meals, baby-sitting, homework, grocery shopping, yardwork, putting toys away, cleaning, or fix-it projects around the house. Encourage everyone to mention at least one chore or struggle that he or she faces.

After five minutes, have families go back to their own tables to work. Instruct each family to create a "coupon book" for its partner family by writing on index cards certain jobs that could be provided to meet the other family's needs. For example, if someone said that he or she needed help painting a fence, one of the children from the partner family might create a coupon that read, "Two free hours of fence painting." Give families ten minutes to work on their coupon creations. Then have families create decorative index card covers for their coupon books, staple the books together, and present them to the partner families.

Challenge families to trade coupons back and forth and to find other ways to serve each other. Families with young children might schedule playtimes at each other's homes. Exchanging baby-sitting allows parents a few minutes for quiet shopping or a night away. Kids can help by cleaning up someone else's room for a change! It's always more fun when you have help.

....

Taking It Home

Encourage family members to make coupon books for each other. For example, a parent might offer coupons for free room service, a party with friends, snuggle-and-read time, pizza on demand, or a nag-free day. Kids could offer to obey without grumbling, to vacuum the living room, to help wash the car, to serve breakfast in bed, to dry dishes, or to clean the bathroom. As family members redeem coupons, they can suggest other ways to serve each other. There's no limit to ways that we can serve one another.

....

Passport to Adventure

Family Focus: Family members will "travel" through three learning stations to learn how they can "go" into the world.

Supplies: You'll need church maps showing the locations of three learning centers; a passport; staplers; blue construction paper; pens or markers; scissors; white paper; an instant-print camera with film; glue; Bibles; pencils; several world atlases; world maps; a globe; pencils; poster board; a pair of shoes; and toy cars, trains, boats, and airplanes.

Before the meeting, set up the following learning stations:

Station 1. Set out Bibles, pencils, and several world atlases. If possible, hang a world map on the wall. Arrange for a "travel agent" to explain to families what they are to do at this station:

• Each person is to find in an atlas or on the map the most distant place he or she has visited.

• Then family members are to explain why they traveled to those places and list other reasons people travel to other countries.

• Finally, family groups should read Matthew 28:18-20 and Acts 1:8 together and discuss what Jesus wants Christians to do, where he wants them to do it, and how this might involve travel. Everyone should write the answers to these questions in his or her passport.

Station 2. Set out a globe, pencils, poster board, pens or markers, and several world atlases. Ask a travel agent to explain what families are to do at this station:

• The youngest family member should spin the globe, close his or her eyes, and put a finger on the globe to stop it.

• Then family members are to look up in an atlas the country the globe stopped on and learn what they can about it. They might focus on facts such as population, climate, area, primary religion, and the like.

• Finally, family members are to work together to create a poster that presents what they learned in a fun and informative way.

Station 3. Set out pens or markers; poster board; a pair of shoes; and toy cars, trains, boats, and airplanes. Hang a world map on the wall. Arrange for a travel agent to explain what families are to do at this station:

• Family members are to discuss which means of transportation would carry them to these places: across their country, across their continent, and overseas.

• Then family members are to write or draw on the poster board ways they could "go" to those places without leaving home. For example, families might call on the telephone, write a letter, or send an e-mail message.

• Finally, have family members choose one way they will "go" to share God's love with someone in a distant country. Families might send money to a missionary or a helping organization, send Bibles to people who need them, pray for a country, or adopt a family pen pal. Have each person write the chosen way in his or her passport.

Set out the supplies for people to make "personal passports."

When families arrive, give them church maps showing where each learning station may be found. Explain that family members will go through learning stations together to discover how they can "go into the world" with God's love.

Before you let families go, hold up the passport and ask someone to explain what passports are used for. Then point out the passport materials, and invite each person to make a personal passport with a blue construction paper cover and several white pages on the inside. Encourage people to make the passport covers as realistic looking as possible. Use the instant-print camera to take "passport photos" people can glue inside the front covers of their passports.

Family-friendly Advice

For extra fun, set an ink pad and a "fun" stamp at each station so travel agents can stamp people's passports when they complete the station.

After five to ten minutes, ask families to proceed to the stations. Families may spend up to fifteen minutes at a station and then move on to a new station. Ask families to return to your meeting area in forty-five minutes even if they have not finished every station. Then ask family groups to scatter among the stations so no one station becomes overly crowded.

Circulate among the stations, and remind people to move on every fifteen minutes. When forty-five minutes is up, encourage families to return to your meeting area.

When everyone has returned, have each family form a group. Then ask families to report what they learned about their countries and how they can "go" share God's love with the people in that country. Close with a prayer asking God to help families take God's love wherever they go. Encourage people to take home the passports to remind them of their commitment to "go" into the world with God's love.

Taking It Home

Challenge families to talk during the coming week of various ways they can take God's love into their own communities. Suggest that people write their ideas in the passports and then check them off when they put those ideas into action.

Baskets of Blessings

Family Focus: Family members will make baskets of goodies for community workers.

Supplies: You'll need Bibles, index cards, curling ribbon, scissors, decorative tissue or cellophane, individually wrapped candies, newsprint, and a marker. You'll need each family to supply a basket and a home-baked treat.

Have families form small groups around tables. Invite singles to form small groups of four or five. Set out ample supplies on each table for groups to use in preparing their "Blessings Baskets."

Explain that this service project will thank volunteers who help people in the community. Ask people to brainstorm together a list of people who volunteer in your community, such as people who help in a food kitchen or a homeless shelter, volunteer firefighters, or school board members. Record people's ideas on the newsprint.

Then ask family members to read Galatians 6:9-10 together and then discuss the following questions:

- **What good things do these community workers do?**
- **What might life be like if they didn't serve as they do?**
- **Why is it important for us to show appreciation to them?**
- **What are some ways we can show our appreciation to them?**

Then explain that families will make "Blessings Baskets" for the groups on the list to show their appreciation for all that the groups do. Invite each family to choose one category or group from the list. Write each family's name beside its group. If you have more families than groups, add additional groups so that each family has one.

Then instruct families to use the supplies on the tables to create beautiful baskets of goodies for their groups. Encourage families to pick out appropriate passages of Scripture for their groups. If, for example, a family chooses a fire-fighter, members might include Isaiah 43:2. If another family has chosen a volunteer at a food kitchen, its members might want to cite Matthew 25:34-40.

When baskets are complete, ask each family to write a personal note to the group receiving the basket. Make sure that no one signs his or her name, because the baskets will be delivered mysteriously by the pastor or a lay leader. Don't let anyone know who prepared them.

Close by giving each person a piece of candy to remind him or her to "do good" whenever the opportunity arises.

························

Taking It Home
Encourage families to think of other ways to provide blessings for their chosen groups. Have families pledge to find ways to reach out to their groups at least twice a year. Suggest blessings baskets for Christmas and Easter or secret thank you notes. Let families know how important it is for them to pray together for their groups. Who knows? This simple outreach may be just what someone needs to draw closer to God.

························

Ready, Set, Clean

Family Focus: Families will take responsibility for cleaning and repairing rooms in the church.

Supplies: You'll need simple maps of the church, paper, and pencils.

Prior to the meeting, get permission from the appropriate church committee to clean and repair various areas of your church building.

Ask each family to form a small group. Give each group a map of the church and then lead everyone on a tour of the church. Explain that the goal of this session is for each family to choose a room or area they will take responsibility for cleaning and repairing. When your tour is complete, encourage families to decide on the rooms they will adopt.

When each family has selected a room, ask family members to read 2 Kings 22:5-7 together and discuss the following questions:

- Why should we clean up and repair our church building?
- How is taking care of God's church one way to serve God?
- What would happen if we didn't take care of the church?

Encourage families to take paper and pencils and return to their chosen rooms so they can list whatever supplies they will need to clean and repair the rooms. If people have suggestions for ways the rooms could be improved, invite them to write their ideas on their supply lists. Ask families to be back in fifteen minutes and then send them on their way.

When everyone returns, ask families to report what they found regarding the church's need for cleanup and repair. Then encourage the entire group to discuss the suggested improvements, possibly choosing one or two improvements to complete as a group.

If possible, plan a family work-day for sometime within the next few weeks or month. Ask families to come prepared to finish their jobs. (Don't forget to decide who will provide needed supplies: the church or the families.)

When all the families have finished their jobs, take a tour again to view their corporate efforts. Then have the church staff throw a thank you party for the families. Provide simple refreshments and lots of affirmation. Maybe everyone will have such a good time that they'll want to make it an annual event!

....

Taking It Home

Another way to offer service with an obvious reward is by joining together in a service project such as the ones sponsored by Habitat for Humanity. Church families can go together to work on a Habitat house, and everyone will be given an opportunity to help. The work is personally rewarding and it meets the needs of others. Plus, the family time is precious as everyone works together for a common good.

....

Servants for a Day

family focus: Family members will learn how to become each other's "servants" for a day.

Supplies: You'll need Bibles, a timer or a watch with a second hand, paper, pencils, and small paper lunch-bags.

Ask families to form small groups around tables. Invite people whose families are not present to form groups of four or six. Make sure singles' groups are made up of an even number. Set out paper, pencils, and one small lunch-bag on each table.

Ask members of groups to pick partners. If a family has an uneven number of members, allow one threesome. Explain that partners will be playing Commander and Agent. The younger member of each pair will be the Commander first. For two minutes, Commanders are to instruct their Agents to perform whatever "personal services" they would like—as long as those services aren't dangerous or demeaning. For example, a Commander might have an Agent tie the Commander's shoes, rub the Commander's shoulders, brush off the Commander's back, or scratch the Commander's nose. If everyone understands the rules, start the game.

Call time after two minutes and then have partners switch roles. Permit groups with three members to switch roles a third time so each person has a chance to be a Commander.

Then have each family or group read Mark 10:35-45 together and discuss the following questions:

- **Which did you like most: serving or being served? Why?**
- **What makes it difficult for you to serve family members?**
- **Why do you think Jesus says we become great by serving?**
- **How might our home life improve if we all served each other?**

Allow time for discussion. Then have each person take a pencil and a piece of paper. Have each person write down everything he or she would have a servant do during a day if he or she could have a servant. Ask parents or older siblings to help younger children by writing down their ideas for them. When family members complete their lists, have them fold the papers and place them in the lunch bag on the table.

Instruct group members to take turns drawing a paper from the bag. If someone picks his or her own paper, have that person return it to the bag and draw another slip. Encourage everyone to keep the name drawn a secret. Have members read the lists and choose things they can do or items they can provide. During the week, individuals are to try to accomplish as much as possible from the lists without being discovered. If it's impossible to keep it a secret, they are to provide the services humbly and in love.

To send everyone off in the right frame of mind, conclude with a second game of Commander and Agent, but this time, instead of having Commanders tell Agents what to do, have Agents think of ways to humbly and lovingly serve their Commanders.

The next time you meet, ask people to report the different ways they were served, how it felt to serve someone secretly, and how it felt to be served.

....

Taking It Home

Ask the pastor or other employees of the church for a list of things they never have time to do. Approach them in a way that makes them think you need the list for other purposes. Maybe explain that you're compiling a list of impossible tasks. Use the list to secretly serve the pastor and other workers. Hand an assignment to each family or group. Encourage families to work together to accomplish some of what is impossible for the pastor alone. It's a great way to build up the flock without wearing out the shepherd!

....

Night Bloomers

Family Focus: Family members will spend some quality time serving others in secret...and at night.

Supplies: You'll need Bibles; note cards (the kind people attach to bouquets work best); pens or pencils; pop bottles; crayons; ribbon; masking tape; scissors; and cut flowers such as carnations, mums, and daisies.

As people arrive, hand each person a cut flower. Ask families to form small groups. Encourage people whose families are not present to join a family group.

Explain that the meeting will prepare people for a secret service project in which they "shower" certain people with flowers. Ask for several volunteers to tell the entire group about times they received "secret" gifts. Encourage volunteers to tell what they received and how it made them feel to be given a gift but not know who gave it.

After three or four people share, have groups read Matthew 6:1-4 and discuss the following questions:

- **Why do you think it's important to do good deeds in secret?**
- **What might happen if other people knew about our good deeds?**
- **What are the benefits of doing good deeds without being seen?**

Then explain that the members of each group are going to work together to make a special bouquet of flowers to secretly deliver to someone after the meeting. Instruct each group to decorate a pop bottle by tearing off small pieces of masking tape and overlapping them until they cover the bottle. Then groups are to color over the masking tape with one color of crayon so the edges of the tape create a wonderful design! Encourage each group to write an encouraging note and then tie the note to the neck of the "vase" with ribbon. Groups may want to write the words to Scripture verses on the notes. Finally, have group members arrange their flowers in the vase and decide who will receive their "secret flower shower." Groups might give the bouquet to residents of a care center, people in the church or community who need to be cheered, or members of the church staff.

Family-Friendly Advice

A fun variation of this activity is to send out "night bloomers" to plant flowers in a park or at a care center, a hospital, or a community center. Make sure you ask the appropriate authorities for permission before you go on your secret mission.

When the bouquets are finished, instruct family members to go together to deliver the bouquet, making sure they are not seen when they make the delivery. If possible, have all the groups deliver their bouquets at the same time and then meet at a restaurant for a late-night snack or an early-morning breakfast. Then send everyone off with a prayer and a reminder to do their good deeds in secret.

Taking It Home

Encourage families to practice secret "random acts of kindness" on a regular basis. For example, a family might leave a pan of hot cross buns on someone's doorstep early Easter morning or secretly deliver a "bouquet" of balloons to a child at school.

Encouragement Theater

Family Focus: Families will work together to create encouraging cassette tapes to send to missionaries or shut-ins.

Supplies: You'll need paper, pencils, markers, blank cassette tapes, and cassette recorders. You may want to ask families to bring their own recorders. You'll also need addresses and pictures (if possible) of shut-ins and missionaries and a bulletin board or poster board.

Before the meeting, post the pictures and addresses of possible "service targets" on a bulletin board or poster board. Set up a room that will act as a "sound studio" for recording the messages.

Have family members form small groups, making sure to include singles and couples in their groups. Provide a cassette recorder and a blank cassette tape for each group.

Set out paper, pencils, and markers at each table. Explain that the goal of this activity is to provide encouragement tapes for shut-ins, members who are ill, and church-sponsored missionaries. Give basic background information for each person listed on the board. Then ask members of each group to choose one person with whom they have common interests, a common background, or whose needs they want to meet. Hand each group the address slip for its service target.

When every group has a service target, have families list Bible verses, songs, and greetings they want to include on the cassette tape. Make sure each person plans a contribution for the tape. Then let families take turns going to the sound studio and recording five to ten minutes of "Encouragement Theater" on their tapes.

Once the tapes are complete, have families form circles to pray for the people who will receive their tapes. Ask families to hand in their tapes with the address slips attached to them. Mail the tapes to the recipients with notes from the church office telling them to stay tuned for the next installment of "Encouragement Theater."

....

Taking It Home

Challenge families to continue their service by "adopting" the people for whom they prepared the tapes. Families can provide tapes, cards, visits, and prayers on a regular basis. To ensure ongoing connection, create a bulletin board featuring the family groups and their adopted groups. Cluster the serving families in the center of the board. Place pictures of the missionaries, shut-ins, and other recipients around the outer part of the board with missionaries far away and shut-ins closer. Connect the families to their adopted people with yarn.

....

Advent Service Calendar

Family Focus: Families will focus the pre-Christmas season on serving rather than on receiving by developing and choosing to follow a service calendar.

Supplies: You'll need enlarged photocopies of the calendar on page 60, construction paper, scissors, markers, Nativity stickers, and glue sticks.

Photocopy and enlarge the calendar on page 60. Make one calendar for each family. Then choose a cause to which your church would like to donate funds. For example, you might collect money for a home for troubled teens, a local relief agency, or a Christmas gift to send to a missionary. Announce that this activity will help families prepare a fun way to collect these funds together. If possible, decorate your meeting room with pictures of and information about the cause for which you are raising funds.

Family-Friendly Advice

Instead of making a calendar, have people write each activity on a slip of paper, take the slips home, and place them into a Christmas box or gift bag. (You might even have families decorate their boxes or bags during the meeting.) Family members can draw out one slip each day and do what the slip says.

When families arrive, give each family a calendar page, scissors, a sheet of construction paper, a glue stick, and six Nativity stickers. Explain that family members will work together to create an Advent service calendar that will help raise money for a worthy cause. Tell people about the cause for which you are collecting. If possible, have a representative from that organization tell a little about who it is and what it does.

Then have family members work together to cut out construction paper squares the same size as the boxes on the calendar. Glue a flap along the top edge of each box so family members can open one flap each day. Instruct children to add a Nativity sticker to each box that doesn't list an activity. Then instruct families to write the dates of the four full weeks prior to Christmas on the calendar flaps. Finally, have the entire family work together to decorate the calendar with markers as they would like.

Explain that families are to open one flap each day and follow the directions they find there. On days with Nativity stickers, family members can decide together how they want to serve that day. Close with families praying together for the people who will receive the money and asking God to help each family member learn more about the needs of other people as they gather these funds this Christmas.

....

Taking It Home

Suggest that families create their own service calendars at other times during the year. It's a great way to raise funds for a special project and to help families be aware of other people's needs. You may want to use cross stickers instead of Nativity stickers during other times of the year.

....

Variation:

Instead of giving each family a preprinted calendar, write each activity on a 1½-inch square of paper. Let families choose from activities and arrange them as desired on their calendars. This allows families to be more flexible to do certain activities when their own family schedule allows.

Sunday	Monday	Tuesday	Wednesday	Thursday	Friday	Saturday
Jesus is the light of the world. Pray for people who live in spiritual darkness because they do not know his light.	Some people live in physical darkness today. Give two cents for every window in your home.	Many people cannot afford glasses. Give a dime for everyone in your family who wears glasses and a quarter for those who wear contact lenses.	sticker	Jesus also called us "the light of the world." Count the candles in your house. Give a nickel for each one.	"You are the salt of the earth." Give a nickel for each time someone in your family used the saltshaker today.	Many people do not have freedom to worship. Give a dime for each member of your family who went to church this week.
Jesus said, "I am the door." Pray for people who have not yet gone through Jesus to know God.	Some people have no doors on their homes. Give three cents for every door in your home.	sticker	Jesus healed many people while He was on earth. Pray for people who need his healing today.	Give a quarter if you have not been ill this month.	Many people are too sick to work. Give a quarter for each member of your family who worked today.	Make a card for someone you know who is sick. Mail or take it to that person.
Jesus said, "I am the bread of life." Pray for people whose hearts are hungry because they don't know Jesus.	"Give us this day our daily bread." Many people are hungry today. Give a quarter for each loaf of bread in your house.	"I was thirsty and you gave me a drink." Give two cents for every drink you took today, ten cents if it had ice in it.	sticker	Did you eat out this week? Give a dime for everyone who ordered.	sticker	Some people can rarely afford to eat meat. What is the price of a pound of your favorite meat? Give that amount.
When Jesus was born, there was no room for him in the inn. If you stayed in a hotel, motel, or tent this year, give a quarter.	Who slept in a bed last night? Give a nickel for each bed in your home.	sticker	Some people have no heat this winter. Give a quarter if you have a furnace, another quarter if you have air conditioning.	sticker	Jesus said he came to heal the hurting. Pray for those who are sad this Christmas. Give them a phone call, too.	Were you happy today? Try to count how many times you smiled! Give a penny for each smile.

Enrichment Activities

Tied Together With Love

family focus: Families will feel the tug of busy schedules and work together to create calendars that include everyone and honor the family.

Supplies: You'll need Bibles, a ball of yarn or string for each family group, markers, and photocopies of the weekly calendar on page 63. You'll need one weekly calendar for each family, couple, or single who attends.

Ask members of each family to stand in a circle. Encourage those whose families are not present to form groups of four to six. When they are in their groups, give a ball of yarn to one person in each group.

Say: **Whoever is holding the ball of yarn, find the end and hold on to it. Then name one of the first things you do in the morning as you throw the ball of yarn across the circle to someone else—all without letting go of the end of the yarn. This person is to repeat the process of telling and holding onto the yarn while tossing the ball. Continue until everyone in your circle has tossed the ball of yarn and it has returned to the first person, weaving your family group together.**

When groups finish, have them repeat the process. This time, ask people each to name where they usually are during the middle of the day as they toss the yarn ball to someone other than the person they tossed it to the first time. Remind family members not to drop the yarn they are holding but to add a second strand to it.

Repeat the process a third time, this time asking people to state what time they typically go to bed. As before, people are each to toss the yarn ball to someone new.

After the third round, ask family members to follow these instructions without letting go of the yarn (add or substitute instructions that more closely fit your group or community):

- **If you leave home most mornings, take one step backward.**
- **If you regularly shop for groceries, step back from the group.**
- **If you go to school, take one step backward from the group.**
- **If you go to church more than once a week, take a step backward.**
- **If you are involved in any kind of sport, take a step backward.**
- **If you belong to a club or organization, take a step backward.**

Then instruct family members to sit in a circle (without letting go of the yarn) and discuss the following questions. After each question, ask for volunteers to report their groups' responses. Ask:

- **What did you like about this activity? What didn't you like?**
- **How is this activity like your family schedules? different?**
- **What are some time pressures that pull your family apart?**

Ask someone to read aloud Ecclesiastes 2:4-6, 11. Then say: **The Bible teaches us that being busy and having hectic schedules can be frustrating and meaningless. So every now and then, we need to take the time to look at our schedules. We might find that some of what we are doing isn't as meaningful as we thought.**

Give each family a copy of the weekly calendar. You may want to give couples and singles their own copies to complete. Set out the markers, and have each family member choose a different-colored marker. Then have family members take turns coloring in blocks of time that they are away from the family. For example, kids might color in time spent at school, while parents might color in time working at home or some other place. Continue until everyone's usual weekly schedule is represented on the weekly calendar.

Have family members identify times they can set aside to spend together—with no distractions. Encourage families to outline those times with a color not already used. Then have family members talk about time commitments they could do without in order to create more time for family. Encourage each person to try to identify one time during the week that he or she could "give" to the family. Then have family members conclude by asking God to pull them (and their schedules) closer together.

···

Taking It Home

Suggest that family members use the yarn to create a fun reminder of their need to not let their schedules tug them apart. For example, they might make "family friendship" bracelets to keep them close even when they're apart or a wall hanging in which they pound nails into a board in a fun pattern such as a clock and then wrap the yarn around the nails to complete the design.

···

Weekly Calendar

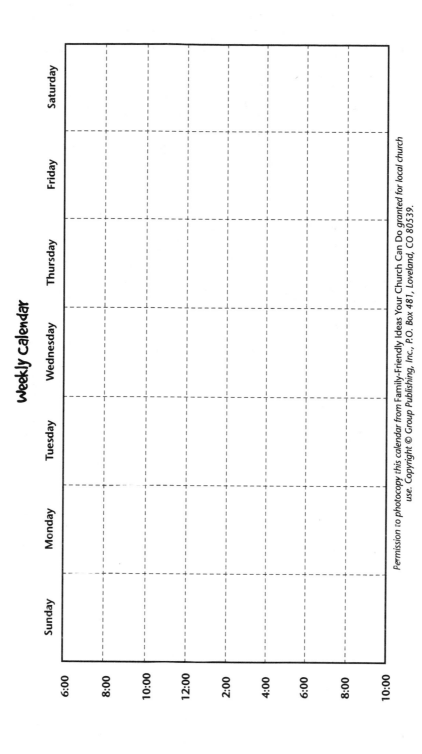

	Sunday	Monday	Tuesday	Wednesday	Thursday	Friday	Saturday
6:00							
8:00							
10:00							
12:00							
2:00							
4:00							
6:00							
8:00							
10:00							

Family Histories

Family Focus: Families will create personal family-histories that will reflect their faith and uniqueness in God.

Supplies: You'll need white paper, construction paper, scissors, glue, pens, crayons, markers, and large book-staplers.

Ask people to form groups of four or five with people other than their family members. Encourage people to form intergenerational groups with children and adults evenly mixed.

Ask everyone to think of his or her favorite personal memory. For example, a child might tell about a family vacation at a theme park, while an adult might recall the birth of a child. Allow one minute of "think time" and then have group members tell each other their memories.

When everyone has shared a memory, have group members discuss the following questions:

- **What did you like about telling others your favorite memory?**
- **Why is it important for us to remember and share good times?**
- **What are some ways we can remember and share good times?**

While people are talking, set white paper, pens, crayons, glue, scissors, and markers at each table. Put the staplers in a central location for all groups to share. After five minutes, ask for volunteers to report their groups' answers.

Instruct family members to form their own small groups. Invite people whose families are not present to form small groups of four to five. Explain that the goal of this activity is for each family to create a personal family-history book. This book can include whatever family members want. Possibilities include how the couple met, wedding memories, births of children, family vacations, holiday celebrations, and casual family outings to the zoo, the park, or the beach.

Give families and groups several minutes to discuss and decide what to include in their books. Instruct families to make notes on what they want to include. Then have family members each agree to take

Family-Friendly Advice

Have members of "unrelated" groups work on individual family-histories they can use to tell others about their family backgrounds. Or encourage group members to discuss how they might show the church's history. Have them pool their knowledge about the church to write a brief history of it, making sure to note when they started attending.

responsibility for a certain aspect of the book. Young children might enjoy illustrating and designing the book. Older children will enjoy writing parts of the story by themselves. Make sure that each person has a special part in the creation of the book. Have the entire family work together to create a construction paper book cover. (For an extra touch, bring an instant-print camera and film. Then take a picture of each family to include on its book cover.)

Allow families twenty to thirty minutes to work on their books. Encourage families to talk about how God was working in their lives during these "memorable" times. When families finish their history books, help each one staple its book together. If you have time, ask each family to share one or two memories with the rest of the group. Conclude in prayer, thanking God for the gifts of memory and family and asking God to help each family cherish its special memories and to create many more new ones.

Consider displaying the family-history books in the church for a week or two. What a wonderful way to "advertise" your fun family ministry events!

Taking It Home

Encourage families to take this idea even further at home. Families can use photographs, meaningful documents, personal illustrations, and encouraging notes to create memorable birthday, graduation, or wedding presents. Remind families to weave God's working in their lives into the story line of each book. These keepsakes will hearten family members for years to come.

Service Dinner

Family Focus: Families will serve each other and discover the joy of meeting the needs of others.

Supplies: You'll need Bibles, paper plates, plastic tableware, napkins, candles, and food of your choosing.

Prior to the meeting, set up your meeting room for a meal. The standard arrangement of tables and chairs is easiest. However, this experience can be enhanced by using folding tables with their legs folded and the tables placed on the floor. Or you can simply arrange tablecloths right on the floor. Everyone sits on the floor with these last two options, which allows younger children and adults to be on the same level.

Before people arrive, prepare your food in sufficient amounts for everyone. This activity can replace a meal or serve as an appetizer before a meal. In any case, arrange serving platters of the food on each table. Several smaller platters of the same items might work better than one platter of each. (If you use tables, you might soften the light in the room by using a candle on each table for light.)

As families arrive, invite each family to select a table (or a spot on the floor). Invite those whose families are not present to sit in groups of six to eight. Several families or groups may share a table, but family members should sit together.

Ask people not to eat anything until you tell them to do so. When everyone is seated, say: **Welcome to our Love Feast. Let's begin with a prayer.** Say a prayer thanking God for the food and then say: **This food has been especially prepared for you. However, to receive this food, you must follow some simple instructions. Since we are families, we care about each other. We watch out for one another. We work together to meet each other's needs. So during this meal, you may not receive any food until someone in your family serves it to you. You may not ask for it in any way. Someone must see your need and offer something to you. You may decline what you are offered, but you can't ask for something else. If you want seconds, it must be offered to you again. This means that even while you eat, you must attend to the needs of others or they won't eat. Those are the rules for our feast. Enjoy your meal.**

Allow fifteen to twenty minutes for people to serve each other and eat. When participants seem generally satisfied with the meal, have them discuss the meal by answering these questions:

- **What did you like about the food you were served? What didn't you like?**
- **How did it feel to wait for someone to serve you? to have to serve others?**
- **How good were you at seeing each other's needs? meeting each other's needs?**

Ask the person in each group who was born closest to August to read 1 Corinthians 12:12-20. Ask:

- **What does the Bible say about our need to work together?**
- **How do we take care of each other's needs in our family?**
- **How might we take care of each other's needs even better?**

Allow time for discussion and then say: **Beginning with the person who has the darkest hair, share one thing you will do to help meet the needs of the family or individuals in the family.** Allow time for sharing and then say: **For our last sharing time, parents, speak to each child in** your family and tell your child what he or she means to you and to your family. (If some people are not with their families, have them each share a memory of a special time with their families.)

Allow time for sharing. This could be an emotional time, so be careful not to intrude on the time. When it seems that groups are finished sharing, close with a prayer. If you are using this as a predinner activity, give the groups a brief break before beginning the main meal.

Taking It Home

Challenge family members to periodically repeat this activity at home. For example, families might designate one night a month as "Service Supper" and take responsibility to prepare and to serve each other a meal. Remind families to be especially attentive so they know exactly how other family members want to be served.

Our Family Tree

Family Focus: Families will learn that everyone plays an important part in the growth of a healthy family.

Supplies: You'll need Bibles, newsprint, markers, glue sticks, green and brown construction paper, scissors, and pencils or pens.

Before the meeting, hang a sheet of newsprint and draw a large outline of a tree on it. Be sure to show the roots underground. Set out construction paper, scissors, glue sticks, and pencils or pens on tables around the room.

As participants arrive, invite them to form family groups. Those who did not come with families should be invited to form groups of four. Say: **Today we're going to talk about our family trees.** Ask:

• **What do you think of when I say "family tree"?**

After several responses, say: **When we talk about a family tree, most people think of a family's ancestors, history, or ethnic roots. But that's not what we're going to talk about today! Instead, we're going to talk about real trees and see how they might remind us of families.**

Direct people's attention to the picture of the tree. Point out the roots, the trunk, the branches, and the leaves. Encourage groups to assign each person a discussion role such as recorder, reporter, timekeeper, or cheerleader. Then tell groups they have one minute to discuss each of the following questions:

- **What do the roots do for a tree?**
- **What does the trunk do for a tree?**
- **What do the branches do for a tree?**
- **What do the leaves do for a tree?**

When groups have had time to discuss the last question, ask for volunteers to report their groups' answers. Record groups' answers on the newsprint. Give every group a chance to report on one or more of the questions.

Say: **These are some great thoughts on trees. Now let's make the connection to families. First, use the supplies at your table to make a "family tree." Be sure to include roots, trunk, branches, and leaves. After several minutes, I'll ask some questions to help you learn how your family is like a tree.**

Allow adequate time for families to create their trees and then ask families to write the endings to the following sentences on their trees:

- **Just as the roots nourish a tree, our family is nourished by...** (Suggest that families name people, family traditions, God's love, their faith, or whatever they think is nourishing to their families.)
- **Just as the trunk provides strength for a tree, our family is strengthened by...**
- **Just as branches reach out from the tree, our family reaches out by...**
- **Just as a tree's leaves offer protection from the hot sun, our family protects itself by...**

While families talk, circulate among groups and offer help as needed. When everyone has finished, read Psalm 1:2-3. Then say: **Put your tree on the floor, join hands around the tree, and then offer a prayer of thanks to God for the living water he gives to your family tree through Jesus Christ.**

....

Taking It Home

Encourage each family to display its tree somewhere at home as a reminder of the many ways God has made the family strong. You might even suggest that family members plant a tree in their yard to remind them that God can help them grow closer and stronger as a family.

....

Hands Around the Room

Family Focus: Family members will create a border of hand prints to affirm each person and connect the entire church family.

Supplies: You'll need Bibles, tempera paints, pie pans, newspaper, wet washcloths, towels, markers, masking tape, and one sheet of construction paper for each person.

Before this activity, place tempera paint in pie pans. Spread newspaper on tables to make cleanup easier. Set the pie pans, construction paper, markers, wet washcloths, and dry towels on tables, one table per family or group.

Ask each family to form a group around a table. Encourage people whose families are not present to form groups of four to five and to gather around tables. Say: **We're going to create a beautiful border by putting our hands together. Using the tempera paint, help one another create hand prints on the construction paper. Make sure both of each person's hands are placed on one sheet. Then use the washcloths and towels to help each other clean up.**

Give groups five minutes to make the hand prints and then instruct groups to set the paintings aside to dry. Have family members hold hands and play a game of affirmation. Say: **Choose someone in your group to begin the game. This person is to look to the person to his or her left and say,** "(Name), **you are** (fill in with the affirmation)." **You might say things such as,** "Daddy, you are kind" **or** "Brooke, you help others." **After you've given the affirmation, describe a special example of that trait. You might say** "Mommy, I remember when you made pancakes last Saturday" **or** "Brooke, thanks for helping carry the groceries last week." **Go around the circle once and then stand up, trade places, and play again with new neighbors.**

Ask family members to change places at least twice. Then say: **Now use markers to write affirmations around each other's hand prints. You can write the affirmations you shared earlier or other affirmations you**

Family-Friendly Advice

Instead of using paper and paint, provide one balloon for each family member. Have people draw their faces on the balloons and then let family members add affirmations. Younger children will especially enjoy the use of balloons. Whether you use hand prints or balloons, this activity is guaranteed "hands down" to "lift" the spirits!

want to give to a family member. Use a variety of colors to make each person's hand print page bright with color.

When families have finished writing out affirmations, ask each family to read 1 Thessalonians 5:11 together and then discuss the following questions:

• **Why do you think it's important to build each other up?**

• **What are other things we can say to build each other up?**

• **What are things we can do to build one another up?**

To close, have everyone stand in a circle and hold hands as you pray: **Lord, as we stand together holding hands, we ask you to bless the members of each family for the wonderful things they bring to our church. Each person here is precious, and our circle simply wouldn't be complete if anyone were gone. Help us to use our hands and our words to build others up and to make each other feel special.** Encourage everyone to shake hands or hug before leaving.

Taking It Home

Suggest that families place the hand prints in a well-traveled area of their homes. Encourage them to keep markers nearby and to write down new affirmations whenever a family member does something nice. It won't be long before families have their "hands full" of good things to say about each other!

Interviews With the Stars

Family Focus: Family members will interview each other to learn why each family member is a real-life "star."

Supplies: You'll need a Bible, paper bags, flashlights, a watch, and fun costume accessories such as feather boas, hats, white gloves, scarves, and funny eyeglasses. You'll also need one pretend microphone for each family. "Microphones" can be anything from a carrot to a pencil. Be creative!

Before this activity, place a few costume accessories, a pretend microphone, and a flashlight in a paper bag for each family or group. Fold the tops of the sacks over so that no one can peek inside.

Ask family members to form small groups. Invite people whose families are not present to form small groups of four with people they don't know very well. That will make this activity even more interesting!

Say: **Today we are going to meet some very special celebrities: each one of you! You will each get to take a turn being a star. You'll have five minutes in the spotlight while the other members of your group ask you ten questions to learn as much as they can about you. Before stepping into the spotlight, choose one prop that expresses your personality from the bag. If you feel like a movie star, pick out some cool sunglasses. If you love to be out in the wild, find a fun hat or scarf. Make your time in the spotlight count by picking the right prop. Also, remember to use a microphone, which you'll also find in your bag. Finally, ask someone in your group to hold the "spotlight" while you speak.**

If everyone understands what to do, have each family choose its first star and begin the interview. Remind people to ask questions that will tell them things they don't already know.

Call time at five minutes and allow each group to choose its next star. When everyone has had a turn at being a star, have groups put the props away. Say: **Now I want you to find another group to match up with. You'll be spending time introducing the members of your group to the other group. Try to pair up with a family or group that you don't know very well. You'll have five minutes to tell as much as you can about each other to the other group.**

After five minutes, have groups switch roles. Then, when groups finish sharing, have them return to their original spots to discuss the following questions. After each question, ask for volunteers to report their groups' answers. Ask:

● **What interesting facts did you learn about the members of your group?**

   ● **What would you like to know more about from a family member?**
   ● **How did it feel to be in the spotlight with everyone listening?**
   ● **How well do you treat each other like important stars at home?**
   ● **What could you do every day to make each other feel like stars?**

Read aloud Philippians 2:3-4 and then say: **When you are at home this week, you can still feel like stars. So pick a special place and time for more interviews. If your family eats breakfast together, plan on having interviews to see how everyone is doing one morning a week. Or parents, maybe you want to check on your "stars" before you tuck them in** at night. Whatever you do, be sure to keep getting to know each other and treating each other like the stars that you are.

··

Taking It Home

Invite families to take home their pretend microphones. Encourage them to conduct more in-depth interviews at the dinner table or before bed. Remind families to allow only one star in the spotlight at a time and to listen carefully while a star is being interviewed. Kids will enjoy being the center of attention, and parents will have the wonderful opportunity of getting to know their kids better.

··

Code Bugs

Family Focus: Families will identify problems that "bug" them and devise code words to help them deal with the real issues.

Supplies: You'll need index cards and fine-tipped permanent markers.

Place the index cards and the fine-tipped markers on tables. You'll need at least one index card per person and a colorful selection of markers for each group.

Have members of each family gather around a table. Say: **Although we don't always want to admit it, every one of us gets "bugged" by certain things that family members do. Parents are sometimes bugged by their kids' tastes in music or clothes, while kids are often bugged when their parents tell them about how life was when *they* were growing up. These bugs probably won't go away, so instead of just ignoring them, we need to talk about them and maybe even laugh about them. So let's have some fun as we tell each other what really bugs us.**

Instruct family members each to think of one thing that someone in the family does that bugs him or her. Then have family members take turns acting out the "bugs" they've chosen. Remind family members to role play the bugs with a spirit of love and fun—without hurting anyone's feelings. While one person is acting out a bug, other family members are to try to guess what is being acted out.

When everyone has acted out a bug, have each person write his or her bug

on an index card and then draw a picture of a real bug on the same side of the card. Permit several minutes for people to complete their drawings.

After everyone has a picture of a bug and a description of what bugs him or her, explain that family members are going to become Secret Code Agents to learn how to handle these problems in a fun and effective way. Have families discuss code words that will help them discuss each problem calmly whenever it arises. Explain that each problem is based on how someone in the family acts. If a child feels that he or she is always being nagged, the person nagging needs to find creative alternatives to nagging. If a mother is bugged by a son's recklessness, the son needs to remember why his mother gets upset. Families are to think of code words to help them discuss and deal with each bug. For example, a son might choose "eagle" as his code word. This code word would remind the mom that one day her little boy will fly away, so allowing him to spread his wings a little now is important. The mom, however, might choose "guardrail" as her code word to remind the son that she wants him to be careful because she loves him.

Allow families plenty of time to discuss their code words and to draw or write their codes on the backs of their index cards. Remind family members that they must be willing to work together to think up their code words and to make them work. When a son says "eagle" or holds up his card, a mom may need to stop nagging and remind her son that she cares for him and for his safety. In a similar way, a son should take his mother's "guardrail" warning seriously and alter his actions accordingly.

Encourage the younger kids in the group to keep their cards with them at all times. Whenever the situations come up that bug them, have them pull out their cards and hold them up. Encourage parents to respond by taking time out to talk through problems.

Once everyone has drawn or written out a code word, ask family members to form circles, join hands, and pray that their secret code words will help to "debug" their families.

Give out fly swatters at the end of the meeting. Although the humor is obvious, the swatters will also act as a reminder to work out the "bugs" for better communication. Invite each family member to take the fly swatter to another family member when he or she really feels bugged. Then, while holding the fly swatter, the two can pray for God's help in getting rid of the pesky bugs.

Our Family Legacy

Family Focus: Family members will create a coat of arms to portray what's special about their family.

Supplies: You'll need a half-sheet of newsprint and colored markers for each family. (If possible, contact families ahead of time and ask them to bring their own markers.)

Ask each family or couple to gather around a table. Invite singles to form trios and to work alongside their trio members. Give each family or single a half-sheet of newsprint. Set the colored markers where everyone can use them. Explain that the goal of this activity is to create coats of arms that portray what's important about each family represented. Families and couples should portray their current families; singles can create coats of arms for either their families of origin or the families they've already raised.

To get started, have each family, couple, and single draw the outline of a coat of arms on the sheet of newsprint. (See illustration.) Then ask family members and trio members to list the characteristics that make their family

special. Encourage people to be honest as well as positive. For example, people might talk about how family members are loyal to each other during difficult times, how they forgive one another for past wrongs, or how the family is a place of peace in the midst of chaos.

After several minutes, have families and trios discuss how to depict those characteristics on their coats of arms. For example, a lion in the center of a coat of arms might represent family loyalty, open hands might portray forgiveness or acceptance, and a yellow and blue background might depict family warmth and peace. Encourage families to creatively think up and then draw things that they think portray their special traits. Make sure everyone leaves room to add one symbol for each family member later on.

After ten to fifteen minutes, ask families to list the traits that make each person a valuable member of the family. (Trio members can tell each other about the members of their actual families.) When every family member has been talked about, have families and trios discuss how they could represent everyone's special traits on the coat of arms. For example, families might use a heart to portray a loving family member or a sun to represent a family member who brings warmth and smiles to the family.

Allow families ten to fifteen minutes to talk about and draw each family member's special contributions and then have each family show and explain its coat of arms to another family. Encourage everyone to brag on his or her family just a little.

To close, have each family or trio thank God for the special things that each family member brings to the family. Encourage families to take their coats of arms home as a reminder of the special strengths of their families and family members.

Family-Friendly Advice

Instead of having families take home their coats of arms, tape them together into a huge "family quilt." Then display the family quilt in the church worship area during special family events or times. You might even invite families who are new to the church to create their own coats of arms and then add them to the church family quilt.

Taking It Home

Suggest that families display their coats of arms in other ways. For example, someone might paint or decorate the family's coat of arms on wood and then cover it with varnish to create a beautiful wall-hanging. Or a family might transfer the coat of arms onto the backs of T-shirts and write family members' names on the front.

Family Mission Statements

Family Focus: Family members will create a "mission statement" that outlines their family's corporate goals.

Supplies: You'll need Bibles, paper, pens or pencils, and logos from sports teams, fast-food restaurants, well-known products, and nonprofit organizations. Be sure that some logos are for kids' products and some are for products geared toward adults.

Family-Friendly Advice

This activity offers an excellent follow-up to "Our Family Legacy" (p. 74). After family members make a coat of arms to portray their family strengths in "Our Family Legacy," they'll be ready to discuss how they can shape those strengths into family goals, which is the purpose of this activity.

Begin by showing everyone the logos. Invite people to call out the name of the team, company, restaurant, or nonprofit organization for which each logo stands. After you've shown all the logos, explain that many businesses have mission statements that tell exactly what the business wants to do. For example, the mission statement for a fast-food restaurant might be "to deliver tasty food for a reasonable price in a short amount of time." If everyone understands what a mission statement is, hold up several of the logos and ask people to suggest what the missions of those companies might be.

After you've displayed and discussed the logos, ask families to form small groups and discuss the following questions:

- **Why do you think businesses create mission statements?**
- **Why do you think these teams and businesses have logos?**
- **How are the logos related to the purposes of these places?**
- **What do you think our family's mission or goal should be?**

Then explain that, just as mission statements help companies remember why they are in business, mission statements can help families remember why they are together. So families are going to spend the rest of their time together creating family mission statements that will help family members make sure that they're all working toward the same goals.

Give each family several sheets of paper and a pen or pencil. Then have family members write various things they would like to be true of their family. Encourage each family member to offer at least two ideas. For example, families might write, "We would like to take one family excursion every week" or "We would like to 'adopt' one child being helped by a relief agency."

After five to ten minutes of discussion, ask a volunteer to read aloud Mark 12:28-31. Explain that the goal of every Christian is to serve God and others, so families are to write these headings on a second sheet of paper: "Serving God," "Serving Others," and "Serving Each Other." Then have family members choose from their earlier lists one way they will serve God, others, and each other and write each idea under the appropriate heading.

Allow five minutes for people to work and then explain that families have just developed their own family mission statements. The three headings outline the general mission of the family, and the specific ideas state how they will accomplish their mission. Then encourage family members to pray together, committing their family to work toward its mission and asking God to help the family expand and adapt the mission as he leads them to do so.

....

Taking It Home

Suggest that family members write their mission statement on parchment and hang it in a frame where they'll see it often. Encourage families to periodically review the details of the mission statement to evaluate how well they're doing and to see if God would like them to expand or adapt it in some way.

....

Family Shuffle

Family Focus: Family members will switch roles to learn how they can communicate with and understand each other better.

Supplies: You'll need paper, pencils, a watch, and photocopies of the "Family Conferences" handout on page 80.

Before the meeting, make one copy of the "Family Conferences" handout (p. 80) for every five people.

As people arrive, have them sit together in family groups. Invite people whose families are not present to join family groups. Then say: **There's an old saying that says if you want to understand someone, you need to walk a mile in his or her shoes. Discuss with your group members what you think that saying means.**

After a minute, ask for volunteers (preferably children) to report their groups' insights. Then explain that you're going to play a game of Family Shuffle to help everyone experience "walking a mile" in another family member's shoes. Adults will experience how it feels to be a child, maybe having little or no control over what the family does, while children will play adult roles and discover what it's like to take adult considerations into account.

Have people form new groups of four or five, with at least two adults and two children in each group. Make sure participants aren't with their own family members. Then ask groups to form circles, facing inward. Explain that for the next twenty minutes each group will act as a family.

To assign family roles, have the youngest group member become the father; the next youngest person, the mother; the next youngest person, a seventeen-year-old son; the next youngest person, an eleven-year-old daughter; and the oldest person, a five-year-old-daughter. In groups of four, omit the role of the seventeen-year-old son and assign the other roles as described above.

Encourage participants to have fun with the game and their roles but to be realistic. An eleven-year-old daughter has very real concerns in any family meeting, so characters playing that part should attempt to represent them. A parent has concerns, too, and those characters should keep them in mind.

Explain that "families" will work together to solve a problem or to make a decision. In the process, people will experience what it's like to be in each other's shoes and gain insight into the pressures other family members may feel. Tell families they have twenty minutes to resolve their issues and then they'll all discuss their experiences.

Give each family a sheet of paper and a pencil. Then assign each family one of the situations from the "Family Conferences" handout (or other situations you have created). Remind people that they have twenty minutes to resolve their issues. Then give five-, three-, and one-minute warnings so groups can wrap up their discussions.

When time is up, ask families to report their conclusions to the rest of the group. Then have everyone rejoin his or her real-life family and discuss the following questions. After each question, ask for volunteers to report their groups' answers. Ask:

- **What did you enjoy about this game? What didn't you enjoy?**
- **What did you learn about other family roles from this game?**
- **How can you apply what you learned to your real-life family?**

To close, ask family members to exchange shoes so each child is wearing at least one adult shoe and each adult has his or her toes tucked into at least one child's shoe. Then invite family members to close in prayer, asking that God help them remember what it's like to be in other family members' shoes.

Taking It Home

Suggest that family members "reverse roles" from time to time to help them remember what it was like to be in other family members' shoes. Parents might give kids responsibility for planning a family outing or kids might assign chores to parents for a day or a week.

Family Conferences

- Discuss and decide on a family policy regarding bedtimes. Who, if anyone, should have one? When should they be? What happens if someone wants to stay up later? Are there any exceptions? If so, what are they?

- Discuss and decide on a family policy regarding chores. Who is responsible for what? Are younger kids expected to do as much work as older kids? What happens if someone doesn't do his or her chores? Can someone pay someone else to do his or her chores? If so, under what circumstances?

- Discuss and decide how much allowance each family member is to receive. Does everyone receive the same amount? If so, why? If not, how much should each person receive? Are there any conditions for receiving an allowance? Are there limits on how each person can spend his or her allowance?

- Decide where you'll go on a family vacation. The vacation will take you away from home for three weeks. Where will you go? How will the vacation affect your schedules? How much money will you spend? How will you travel?

Fun Times

Round-'Em-Up Rodeo

Family Focus: Families will enjoy a taste of the Old West in a rodeo for all ages.

Supplies: You'll need ½-inch-by-4-foot dowel rods (or old broom handles), clean white socks, newspaper, duct tape, tacky craft glue, felt, scissors, markers, one-foot-square pieces of cloth, permanent markers, brown construction paper, supplies for the rodeo events you choose (see below), barbecue sandwiches (or hot dogs), chips, drinks, haystack desserts (see below), plates, cups, and napkins.

Set socks, newspaper, duct tape, tacky craft glue, scissors, dowel rods, felt, and markers on one table. Put the cloth squares and the permanent markers on another table. Use brown construction paper to create one "tail" for each family.

To make haystack desserts, melt together one large package of milk chocolate chips and one large package of butterscotch chips. Mix in a large bag of crunchy chow mein noodles. Then put spoon-sized dollops of the mixture on a foil-lined cookie sheet. Cool in a refrigerator until the haystacks are firm. This will make approximately two dozen haystacks.

To begin, explain that families will compete in a number of rodeo events. Of course, to compete in a rodeo, people need horses. So have family members work together to create a horse for each person. To make a horse, wad up newspapers and stuff them into a sock until it is full. Then tape the open end of the sock to a dowel rod so it looks like a horse's head. Cut

Family-Friendly Advice

The Round-'Em-Up Rodeo is a great way to get families "rounded up" for your other family ministry activities.

out and glue on eyes and ears. Use markers to add a mouth.

When everyone has a horse, have family members mosey over to the table with the bandanna supplies. Have family members choose a family brand, symbol, or design and then decorate one bandanna with that emblem for each family member. Encourage everyone to write his or her first and last names on his or her bandanna.

When everyone is fully outfitted, have families compete in fun rodeo events. Create your own rodeo activities, or use some of the following:

Barrel Races: Use chairs, wastebaskets, or pylons to create two S-shaped courses that rodeo riders can weave in and out of. Have equal-sized families compete against each other in barrel-race relays. If necessary, have one or more people race twice to equalize family teams.

Calf Rope: Give each family a rope with a loop at one end. Ask for one volunteer from each family to be a pretend "calf." Have other family members stand ten to fifteen feet from the calf (closer for younger kids) and take turns attempting to rope it. The family that ropes the calf the most times in two minutes wins.

Stick-Horse Races: Have people form groups according to age: up to five, six to eleven, twelve to seventeen, eighteen to thirty, and over thirty. Have each age group race around the perimeter of your rodeo "arena." Explain that contestants must "gallop" just like a horse (no running) and must slap their "back pockets" as they race. (Kids will love watching their parents compete in this rodeo event.)

Brand the Steer: Ask each family to draw its brand on an index card and cut out the brand. Give each family a tail. Put tape on the brand and the tail so family members can tape them to a "steer." Have one member of the family (preferably a parent) volunteer to be the steer that family members will "brand." Blindfold the other family members, and have them take turns attempting to brand the steer and tape its tail in the right location.

When everyone seems tuckered out from the rodeo events, invite family members to a closing "cookout" in which you serve chips, barbecue sandwiches (or hot dogs), drinks, and haystacks. Then ask family members to help clean up before they ride off into the sunset together.

....

Taking It Home

Suggest that family members continue the rodeo theme by attending a real rodeo or going on a horseback ride together. Encourage families to dress up like real-life cowboys and cowgirls for these excursions.

....

Family Video Night

Family Focus: Families will dress up in costume and be videotaped lip-syncing television theme songs.

Supplies: You'll need a video camera, a video projection unit, a CD or cassette tape player, CDs or tapes of television theme songs or other songs children will know, the words to each song written on a poster, costumes and props appropriate for the songs selected, and an instant-print camera with film.

Welcome families to your "video studio" with television theme songs playing in the background. Explain that each family will get to star in its very own music video. People whose families are not present may want to group together to form a video team. Point out the posters with the song lyrics written on them, the costumes, and the props. Then encourage family members to choose one song to lip-sync together.

The cooperative process of planning and practicing is a key part of this event, so allow families plenty of time to try on costumes and outfit one another. Part of the fun is allowing children to help their parents look and act out of character. Suggest that families plan out simple motions or pantomimes to go with their songs so they don't end up merely mouthing the song for the camera. For example, if family members choose "Old MacDonald Had a Farm," they might decide on motions for Farmer MacDonald and for each animal mentioned in the song.

When everyone is ready, videotape each family lip-syncing its song. Use an instant-print camera to make a snapshot of each family in action so families will have mementos of the evening. When every family has been videotaped, play your finished "movie" for all the families to enjoy together. For an extra nice touch, serve "movie refreshments" such as popcorn and sodas. Applaud at the end of each video clip and then have families give themselves a rousing round of applause at the end of the movie.

Before people leave, tell families they can borrow the video to replay their own music videos. If you have the capability, offer to make individual copies of the music videos for families that want them.

Family-Friendly Advice

If you want to offer more elaborate props, ask a children's club or a Sunday school class to work together to paint a simple backdrop for each song or to create special costumes. Remind children to invite their parents and siblings to this evening as their special guests.

Taking It Home

Provide a video camera for families to "check out" to create more fun family memories. Periodically invite families to share their family videos with each other. This will promote together-time within families and build relationships between families. For more ideas, see "Funniest Family Videos" (p. 93).

Jungle Safari

Family Focus: Family members will work their way through stations to complete a jungle safari together.

Supplies: You'll need "Jungle Safari" maps showing the location of each station, a poster identifying the name of each station, green crepe paper, tape, "jungle" stuffed animals, any other jungle-related decorations you want, and the supplies listed for each station.

Before your safari, arrange for "guides" to explain to families what to do at the stations. Then set up the following stations:

Safari Cheer. Set out paper, pencils, and a cassette tape recorder with a blank tape in it. Have family members work together to write and record a family cheer or song. Families might want to use the family's last name or each family member's first name in the cheer. If a family has difficulty thinking up a cheer, suggest that members adapt a song or cheer they already know. For example, they could write new words to "The Farmer in the Dell" or create a cheer such as "Give me an S! Give me an M! Give me an I! Give me a T! Give me an H! What does that spell? Smith! Smith! Smith!" Family members might also want to create an acrostic cheer using the letters of the family's last name.

Jungle High Jinks. Set up an obstacle course for family members to navigate together. Use a pup tent, chairs, tables, short ladders, or the church's playground equipment to create the

Family-Friendly Advice

If you'd like, have the guide use an instant-print camera to take pictures of families as they negotiate the jungle obstacles. You might even want to time how long it takes each family to complete the course and then give a prize to the fastest family.

course. Include lots of in, out, over, around, and under movements for families to follow. Climbing, crawling, and jumping add to the challenge. Be creative by adding hanging jungle "vines," "swamps" to cross, or "wild animals" to avoid. Start and finish the course at the pup tent, where families get, and later return, foam safari-hats they must keep on their heads as they complete the course. If a family member's hat falls off, the entire family must return to the beginning and start again.

Adventure Flags. Set out poster board or newsprint, markers, and scissors. Have family members choose an animal mascot and make a family flag with the mascot on it. The animal's name might start with the first letter of a family's last name (such as Larson Llamas) or be an animal that represents a characteristic the family has or would like to develop (such as the Ackley Lions).

Mess Tent. Set out spoons; bowls; ice cream scoops; several types of ice cream and syrups; and various toppings such as granola, chocolate chips, banana slices, colored sprinkles, and cherries. Ask family members to work together to build a family ice cream sundae and then feed it to each other with spoons.

Safari Outfitters. Set out a backpack, ten feathers, and a duffel bag full of safari clothes such as a foam safari-hat, a safari shirt, a scarf, and large short pants. Set the feathers approximately fifteen feet away from the other supplies. (If you can't find feathers, use rocks instead.) Explain that the scientist accompanying your safari has asked families to gather the feathers of a rare bird seen in this area. Family members will take turns dressing in the safari clothes, running to grab one feather, running back to put the feather in the backpack, and then taking off the safari clothes and putting them back in the duffel bag. Explain that the next runner cannot leave until all the clothes are back in the duffel bag. Keep track of how long it takes each family to complete this relay and then post the average time per family member on a chart.

Decorate the entrance to your jungle safari and each station with green crepe paper vines, "jungle" stuffed animals, boxes on which you have printed "Safari," and the like.

As people arrive, give each family a "Jungle Safari" map. Invite families to start wherever they want and to go through the stations in whatever order they choose. Simply remind families to return to your meeting area at a designated time.

When everyone returns, have families display and explain their Adventure Flags. Then play the tape with the Safari Cheers on it. If you want, end your time by awarding fun, safari-related prizes to the families that completed the Jungle High Jinks obstacle course and the Safari Outfitters relay fastest.

Family-Friendly Advice

Other station ideas include putting out objects such as pine needles, bug repellent, sunscreen, lemon, and cloves in baby-food jars for people to identify by smell; providing bath-towel "nets" for people to try to throw over "jungle" stuffed animals; or videotaping family members imitating a family of monkeys.

Sundae Rain

Family Focus: Families will have fun creating a delicious and unique ice cream treat together.

Supplies: You'll need a ten-foot section of new plastic rain-gutter, aluminum foil, markers, ice cream scoops (one per family group), one gallon of ice cream for every four family groups, assorted ice cream toppings, whipped cream, bananas, bowls, and spoons.

Family-Friendly Advice

This activity is a fun way to end a potluck dinner, a church picnic, or another more traditional church-gathering for families. You might also set up this activity on the lawn and use it to close a Vacation Bible School family night or a summer evening worship service.

Set two full-size tables end to end. Place the plastic rain-gutter down the center of the tables. Line the rain gutter with aluminum foil, and mark off one-foot sections of the gutter. If you're expecting more than forty people, set up a second gutter. Set out the scoops, toppings, bowls and spoons, and (just as everyone arrives) the ice cream. You might also want to put a paper or plastic dropcloth under the tables to simplify cleanup.

As people arrive, invite those who did not come with a family to form groups of four to six. Assign each group a one-foot section of the rain gutter. Say:

Today we're going to create a giant ice cream sundae. You are encouraged to express yourself freely as you design your section of the sundae. Each group gets to create one foot of our giant sundae. Allow each member of your family group to contribute something to the finished product. When the sundae is finished, we will all have a chance to sample each other's creativity.

Point out the ice cream, the scoops, and the toppings—then let everyone get to work. Allow plenty of time for groups to create the sundae. When everyone is finished, say: **Before our creation melts all over the floor, let's dig in. Feel free to sample the variety of selections that have been created!**

Invite families to use ice cream scoops to load up the various "gutter goodies" into their bowls.

When everyone has had enough sundae, encourage people to dish any leftovers into the ice cream containers to enjoy later at home. Then encourage everyone to help clean up the mess. Be sure to keep the gutter in a clean place for your next "Sundae Rain."

Taking It Home

Invite family members to cooperatively create dinner one night a week. For example, family members might divide up the different steps for making tacos and have one person complete each step. Or suggest that family members each take responsibility for one part of a meal, such as the predinner salad, the main course, dessert, and drinks. For extra fun, have family members keep what they're preparing a secret!

Treasure Hunt

Family Focus: Family members will follow clues leading them around the church and discover the treasure of a hidden dessert at the end.

Supplies: You'll need lists of clues to lead families around the church, plastic coins, a dessert, and eating utensils.

This treasure hunt is tons of fun and helps families visit places within your church building that they might not normally see. Before the meeting, create a list of clues that will lead families around the church. Think up your own clues, or use the following ideas:

• Find water that's not to drink. This water is used for a special reason—to show people we belong to Jesus.

• Someone in our church reads and prays in order to tell us every Sunday what God says in his Word. Find the place where this person prays and writes those sermons.

- Pennies, nickels, dimes, quarters, and dollars—we bring money to God's house. Ushers use these things to collect that money. How many are there?
- Our church building has a birthday! When can it be? How old is our church today? Find the place that tells the date.
- The biggest copy of God's Word—where can you find it open each week? To which book of the Bible is it open?
- Hands and feet work together to make music. How many rows are there for hands to play?
- It's time for church, but what time should we go? Find a place that tells you when church starts.

Be sure that the last clue on your list directs people to the place where you'll be serving dessert. Then set plastic coins (at least one coin for each family you expect) at each of the places families will visit. Finally, prepare and set out the dessert (and any needed eating utensils) in your final treasure spot.

When people arrive, give each family a copy of the clues. Explain that families will be going on a "treasure hunt" to collect coins and to learn more about the church building. Family members must stay together on their hunt, and they can find the clues in any order they choose—as long as they leave the final clue for last. Every time a family solves a clue to find a place, they are to take one coin to show they they've visited that place. When families have visited all but the last place described by the clues, they are then to find the final place, where they will receive a special treasure.

If everyone understands the rules, send families off to hunt for their treasures. Then, when everyone discovers the final spot, serve them all the "treasure" of a delicious dessert.

Taking It Home

Encourage family members to hide the coins around the house—especially in places that need cleaning. If someone finds the coin while cleaning, he or she can redeem that coin for a favorite dessert. Family members may also want to read Matthew 6:21 together and then talk about where their family's treasure really is.

Service Scavengers

family focus: Families will enjoy a progressive dinner as they collect scavenger hunt items to include in care packages.

Supplies: You'll need scavenger hunt lists, markers, mailing supplies, paper, and boxes.

Before the meeting, arrange for three homes, each of which will host one course of a meal for the entire group: one home for salad, one home for the main dish, and one home for dessert. Ask for volunteers to supply food at each home. Create your own scavenger hunt list, or use the following ideas:

- a coupon for a fast-food restaurant,
- a church bulletin from your church,
- a package of hot chocolate,
- a flashlight battery,
- a postage stamp,
- a box or pack of facial tissues,
- a stick or package of gum,
- a homemade cookie or brownie,
- a package of instant soup,
- a plastic bandage, and
- a newspaper ad for your church.

Ask families to gather at the first home to enjoy salad together. After families introduce themselves, encourage family members to share memories of past scavenger hunts by answering the following questions:

- **When have you gone on a scavenger hunt?**
- **What kinds of things were you looking for?**
- **Where did you search to find these items?**
- **What did you like about the scavenger hunt?**

Give each family a list of scavenger hunt items. Explain that each family is to collect scavenger hunt items together as they travel to the homes serving the main dish and the dessert. To avoid families arriving late and delaying the main course or the dessert, set a time limit by which they must arrive at each of the next two homes. Tell people that they may not purchase the items from a store, get any more than two items from any one home, go to the homes serving the progressive dinner, or go into anyone's home. Also, tell families that they must explain that they are collecting items to put in care packages for shut-ins (or some other group you designate).

If families understand the rules, remind them of the time limit and invite them to start their scavenger hunts as soon as they finish their salads.

When everyone arrives at the last home, have families compare what they collected. Consider giving the family that collected the most items a small prize, such as a toy trophy to which you have added the label: "The Great Scavengers." Then box up the items you collected to create care packages for college students away from home or shut-ins. Have each family create a card to include in a box. Prepare the boxes to mail to distant recipients, or ask for volunteers to deliver them to nearby shut-ins (perhaps anonymously). Then end your fun time by enjoying dessert together.

Taking It Home

If possible, have a picture of each care-package recipient to send home with a family. Take an instant-print picture of the family groups to include in each care package. Have each family take home the name of a care-package recipient and agree to pray for that person every night at dinner for at least a month.

STAGE Night
(Sharing Talents And God's Excellence)

Family Focus: Families will share their talents and hobbies with each other.

Supplies: You'll need enough tables to hold people's hobbies, paper, pens or pencils, markers, newsprint, and an auditorium or sanctuary with a good sound system.

Several weeks prior to this event, announce that you're going to be holding a "STAGE Night" in which families will have a chance to present their special talents and hobbies. Explain that families can present their talents through music, skits or drama, poetry readings, creative movement, or some other means. Families can also present their hobbies for others to view and learn about.

Have families sign up well in advance for what they would like to do or display. Arrange for a master of ceremonies to lead this event. This person will run the evening schedule as well as direct families to the various activities going on.

You will want to provide some "at event" activities for families to enjoy after your talent show. For example, have families each use pens or pencils and paper to write out a family song or a family cheer. Or have families each use markers and newsprint to create a family logo or banner.

Family-Friendly Advice

To keep a record of everyone's talents and hobbies, have someone videotape the evening. Then make copies and have them available to families who would like to have them.

Begin "STAGE Night" with the talent-show portion of the program. Then invite everyone to adjourn to the hobby area to learn about each other's hobbies and to complete some of the fun family activities. If you want to include a devotional, ask family members to read James 1:17 together and then to discuss the following questions:

- **What gifts or talents has God given you? your family?**
- **How can we use these gifts or talents to honor God?**

Thank families for sharing their talents and hobbies. Then end in prayer, thanking God for giving such wonderful talents and hobbies to these families.

Taking It Home

Encourage families to hold their own family "STAGE Nights" during which everyone works on one family member's hobby. If someone in a family likes a certain hobby, other family members might enjoy it as well!

"Let's Make a Deal"

Family Focus: Family members will dress up in silly costumes, make "deals," and complete fun activities to win prizes.

Supplies: You'll need three large boxes, a marker, and various prizes. Some prizes should be silly (a tube of toothpaste, a can of creamed corn, or an old newspaper); some should be serious (a gift certificate to a local restaurant, a CD or cassette tape of a Christian artist, or a pass to a local amusement park). You'll also need supplies for the games you choose. (See the following game suggestions.)

Before the meeting, number the boxes 1, 2, and 3. Arrange for a master of ceremonies to lead the event and an assistant to put the prizes in the boxes. When you announce the event, ask families to show up in costumes. If possible, family members' costumes should relate to the same theme, such as the characters in a nursery rhyme or a cartoon strip. Explain that you'll be asking for specific items, so each family should bring a bag full of odds and ends that they think you might request.

As people arrive, have family members sit together. Have the master of ceremonies welcome everyone and explain that families will be asked to provide specific items. If a family has an item, the entire family will come forward and try to win a prize by completing a simple activity. If everyone understands, ask for items until there are three families standing at the front. Ask for items such as:

- a family picture,
- the youngest person,
- a 1987 penny,
- a needle and thread,
- a roll (or piece) of toilet paper,
- an adhesive bandage,
- someone born in 1990,
- the most family members,
- a postage stamp, and
- the fewest total number of letters in family members' first names.

Then explain that the three families will compete for the right to select a prize. Have families complete fun competitions such as:

Balloon Pop. Challenge families to see which family can blow up and pop ten balloons fastest.

Family Food-Fest. Blindfold one family member, and ask him or her to feed a piece of pie (gelatin and pudding also work well) to another family member. Encourage other family members to offer directions. The family that feeds the pie best (or fastest) wins.

Water Brigade. Have families compete to see which family can fill a bowl with water fastest. Family members must carry the water in a spoon and pass the spoon off in relay fashion.

Home Sweet Home. Challenge family members to build a house of cards that is six inches tall. Everyone must add cards to the house. The family that finishes first wins.

If necessary, repeat these games or think up your own. Whenever a family wins a game, allow the family to select a hidden prize from one of the three boxes or another prize (such as a cake) that you show them. Rotate the prizes

family-friendly Advice

Encourage the master of ceremonies to use this event to help people learn a little more about each other. When families come forward, the master of ceremonies can ask questions such as "How old are you?" "Where do you live?" "How many pets do you have?" "What school do you attend?" "What is your favorite place to eat?" and "If you added all your ages, how old is your family?"

after each game so people don't know which boxes contain good prizes and which contain goofy ones.

After each game, have the three families return to their seats and ask for items until you have enough families for another round. Keep playing until every family has competed in a game or won a prize.

Taking It Home

Encourage each family to designate one night a week as "Family Game Night," during which family members play various board and card games together. Remind parents to play games that even younger children have a chance of winning.

Funniest Family Videos

family focus: Families will videotape each other in "just for fun" skits and then view each other's funny home videos.

Supplies: You'll need several video cameras, blank videotapes, a video projection unit, dessert, eating utensils, and twenty to twenty-five fun props people can use to create skits. For example, you might use props such as a loaf of bread, a can of tennis balls, chairs, a television remote control, a picnic basket, a sports jacket, a tie, a hat, and a flying disc.

About one month prior to this event, announce that families have an opportunity to submit their videos for a "Funniest Family Videos" night. Explain that families can submit videos in these categories: Baby Bloopers, Family Fun Times, Pet Tricks, Super Sports, and Mad Miscellaneous Moments. Announce also that each family will make its own video on the night of the event.

When people arrive, place two or three families together. Explain that these family teams will work together to tape fun family skits in one of the following categories:

- our latest vacation,
- a family shopping spree,

You can simplify your preparations by announcing the categories of videos families will create and then asking each family to bring its own props to the event. Families may also want to plan their video skits beforehand and then present them "live" to the entire group while someone else tapes them.

- getting ready for church,
- a picnic in the park,
- mealtime madness, or
- a family video night.

Encourage families to choose one category (or one of their own) for which they will prepare a five-minute skit to share a fun family memory with everyone else. For example, a family might choose "our latest vacation" and present a skit about an amusing incident that happened on vacation. Point out the props, and encourage families to choose whatever props they need to create the skit.

Allow families five to ten minutes to plan their skits. Then give each group of families a video camera and encourage them to find a private place to film. Tell people they have thirty minutes to film their skits, after which everyone will return to view the videos previously submitted.

When everyone returns, show the "Funniest Family Videos." If you want, have everyone vote for the funniest video in each category and then present fun prizes to winning families. Then, as the person running the video projection unit prepares the skit videos, play a simple game such as Simon Says or Charades.

After several games, invite everyone to enjoy dessert. Then sit back and enjoy each other's video skits of fun family memories.

Taking It Home

Invite families to spend time during the coming weeks viewing their family videos or looking through family photo albums. Encourage people to remember fun times together and to take turns sharing what was special about each memory.

Family-Fun Covenant

Family Focus: Families will plan to have fun by creating a covenant in which they agree to enjoy certain activities together.

Supplies: You'll need Bibles, paper, pencils, markers, tempera paint, damp paper towels, displays advertising family activities, and lists of various family activities.

This event provides an enthusiastic kickoff to a family summer. In many cases, busy family members would engage in an activity together if the planning were already done for them and the times, prices, and places were already known. Instead of just encouraging families to spend time together, you can do the research to put this information at their fingertips and then help them commit to carrying through with these activities during the summer.

Prior to the kickoff event, research local activities that families can do together. If possible, include activities that would be a little out-of-the-ordinary for your church family. For example, don't list the park where everyone always picnics; choose one that isn't quite as familiar. Gather information for several categories. For example, suggest fairs and free concerts for community activities, parks and hiking trails for outdoor activities, picnics and family programs for church activities, places to visit for local tourist activities, and fun ideas such as family game night, reading a book together, working on a hobby, and looking through photo albums for family activities. Try to list a number of ideas for each category.

Display the information you've gathered on colorful bulletin boards, advertisements, or even video clips—one for each category. Place the categories in different areas of the room. Provide pencils at each category display.

When families arrive, give each family a "shopping list" of the activities you've collected. Have family members each circle their first and second choices for the family to do from each category.

Allow time for families to view the displays and then have members of each family form a group.

Family-Friendly Advice

Set up a bulletin board in the church where families can post photos from their summer covenant activities. Then end the summer with a covenant celebration, giving each family time to share their pictures (and possibly videos) and to advertise to other families what they enjoyed most about these family activities.

Have family members read James 1:19 together and then put this verse into action as they listen to one another tell which activities they would like to do. Remind family members to listen to each other carefully and not to insist on their own way as they negotiate a list of activities the family agrees to do. Ideally, this family agreement will include at least one activity from each family member.

Set out paper, markers, pencils, tempera paint, and damp paper towels. When families have agreed on their lists, have them create their own "Family-Fun Covenants." Suggest that a parent or an older child in each family write "As a family, we agree to..." at the top of the covenant and then list the activities under this sentence. Younger kids will enjoy decorating the covenant with markers.

When everyone is finished, have families gather together to share their lists. Then lead everyone in a covenant-signing ceremony. Have each family member "sign" the family's covenant by dipping the tip of his or her index finger in tempera paint, pressing it to the bottom of the covenant, and then writing his or her name under the fingerprint.

Encourage families to display their covenants on their refrigerators so they're not forgotten. Close in prayer, asking God to bless these families and draw them closer to each other and to him through these activities. If you'd like, end with fun refreshments such as make-your-own ice cream sundaes.

Taking It Home

Suggest that families create "Family-Fun Covenant" scrapbooks in which they place photos and souvenirs from their activities. At the end of the summer, families might also put their covenants in their scrapbooks.